T0131497

Rainbows through Cobwebs

Finding Your 'Fabulous' again...and again

Lyn Traill

BALBOA.
PRESS
A DIVISION OF HAY HOUSE

Balboa Press books may be ordered through booksellers or by contacting:

Balboa Press
A Division of Hay House
1663 Liberty Drive
Bloomington, IN 47403
www.balboapress.com.au
1 (877) 407-4847

Print information available on the last page.

ISBN: 978-1-5043-1695-8 (sc)
ISBN: 978-1-5043-1696-5 (e)

Balboa Press rev. date: 03/04/2019

THE RAINBOW AFTER THE STORM

"Be thou the rainbow in the storms of life. The evening beam that smiles the clouds away and tints tomorrow with prophetic ray." Lord Byron

We are all 'fabulous'. The dictionary definitions of fabulous vary, however, all use the word extraordinary – 'so great we can barely believe it'. I have written on my website that *"It's never too late to find your 'fabulous'."* Even better if we can acknowledge that we have already found it because we **are already** extraordinary beings. I have never met anyone who is not extraordinary, but sadly, I have also met many of us who cannot see the 'fabulous' within ourselves. I have certainly been in that position, and it is now my passion to assist people to uncover or rediscover that extraordinary being lurking within all of us. We all face challenges in our lives that threaten to undermine us and force us to claw our way back. Each time we do this we become so much stronger and even more 'fabulous', again and again, and again!

Grief is no stranger to most people. To some degree, we each experience its dark tentacles reaching into our soul and each of us handles it differently. It is a common saying that each of us grieves in our own way and at our own pace. There are also many circumstances and experiences that cause our grief. I felt moved to write a book that encourages people to know that even in the depths of despair we **can** rise again. We can indeed see our rainbow through the cobwebs of our despair.

How fortunate I have been to have had the opportunity to understand what has been going on for me following my experience of profound grief. I have learnt so much about opening my heart and embracing my feelings. It didn't happen overnight. In fact, had I died at the age my mother did, I would have missed out on learning it at all.

When I wrote my last book, *Sizzling at Seventy – Victim to Victorious*, I was transparent about my struggle to find my true self. Some criticised that transparency as airing my dirty linen, but many identified with my journey and were grateful. At the end of the book, I certainly felt that I had found my 'fabulous' and made a rather arrogant statement that I felt that now I could cope with anything that life threw at me. I will never again make such a statement because life did throw me the biggest curveball of all and I struggled again to once more gain that confidence. I had come so far and had spoken about the strategies that had helped me, yet I found myself stripped bare yet again. Thankfully this time I had more strategies and eventually climbed out of my hole. Having shared my previous journey, I felt moved to share the sequel of my life which has been a profound experience and one that has brought a great deal of learning.

Experiencing deep grief gave me the opportunity to understand the mood that comes with grief and some accompanying emotions such as denial, shock, guilt, and anger. I also found that we tend to look at what we could have done better. My concerns were numerous. Did I show enough love when my husband was suffering? Did I give him the best of me at a time when there was tension in the air? I can now honour the process of grieving and all the learning that comes with it. I learnt that there is no quick fix, no band-aid to put over the gaping wound that is the loss we have experienced. I now understand that the sadness we feel over a loss may never go away and can creep up unawares when a particular song is played, or a thought is triggered by an event. The notion that time heals I believe is erroneous.

The most valuable lessons have been about how to be with others who are experiencing grief. I valued those who didn't shy away from my grief and were able to talk to me openly about what I was going through. I certainly learnt that there are many who found this difficult. I hope those who do, may find some encouragement from what I have written in this book. It is harsh, and unhelpful, to be told that you must get over it and move on. I recognise now that people close to me found it hard to cope with my grief. I think what matters most is that you feel you are understood.

Most of all I learnt how to move past my initial stages of grief and look for a higher purpose when often I just longed to join my love. I learnt that between the spaces of heartache there can be incredibly vivid moments of joy. I learnt that I can open my heart in a way I never had before and sincerely encourage others to become their most fabulous selves.

This book is not just about how to deal with grief. It's about how we can move past the grief and the things we've done that we're not proud about. This book is about inspiring you to reach deep down into your soul and find that beautiful something that will ignite the best of you so you can truly find your 'fabulous'.

"The measure of our greatness is in how we stand up after we fall."
Unknown

TABLE OF CONTENTS

CHAPTER 1

Conversations with Mahatma

"Please Mahatma; you are such a wise man, is it possible for me to ever be well again?" I didn't expect an actual answer from Mahatma. He was, after all, assassinated in 1948, and I was conversing with a statue made of bronze which stood on a high pedestal bearing a plaque stating that this was: *Mahatma Gandi, 1869 – 1948*.

Gandhi's effigy stands proudly in a charming little park close to the heart of Canberra, Australia's Capital Territory. I'd written an essay about him so long ago, and now I was sitting at the feet of this great man, begging to be given some answers. At the side was written Gandhi's "Live *as if you were to die tomorrow. Learn as if you were to live forever.*" At that time, I felt I was neither living or learning and was aching for a semblance of harmony that certainly evaded me at that time. Like most of us, I had not escaped challenges in my life. There had been quite a few peaks and troughs but never had I felt this gut-wrenching pain that wrapped itself around every fibre of my being.

Whilst in my conversations with this man of bronze, I had managed to evade being taken away by men in white coats carrying straitjackets, but members of my family were uncomfortable about some of my behaviour. My son, Simon, had been so concerned he decided that a spell with him in Canberra may help me to regain a semblance of the reasonably rational, optimistic being I had previously imagined myself to be. I was trying hard to get well, attempting meditation; reading stacks of self-help books; eating healthily and now pleading with Mahatma to help me find a way to return to some normality. Despite my efforts, it felt as if it was never going to happen. My friend Gita assured me that I would get well in time and I clung to her promise, but as each day passed, I seemed to sink deeper and deeper into a pit of despair.

The morning when my beloved husband came to show me a golf ball size swelling in his groin, I'd been rather flippant. I think I even said it looked like he'd grown an extra 'ball'. The previous year he had gone under the knife for a hernia from which he recovered very quickly, so at first, I didn't see this latest growth as anything sinister. I had however detected a change in his behaviour over the past year or so. There had been fleeting moments when he seemed to go blank, and after a while, I began to think I imagined them. He was still singing his heart out on stage and managing tasks, albeit more slowly, so I tried not to be concerned. Unfortunately, the doctors' diagnoses confirmed that we were facing something more tangible as the lump had morphed into a melanoma.

I remember the morning I dropped him off at the hospital prior to his operation. We had barely spoken during the drive. It was if we were strangers. There had been a dramatic change in our relationship. My usually gregarious and very loving husband did not want me to be close and certainly did not want me to go into the hospital with him. He quickly hopped out of the car and blew me a perfunctory kiss. I shed a few tears as I waited around for news and was amazed that the first news came via a call from Mick. He was awake and wanted to let me know that he was alright. Although the lump, plus surrounding lymph glands, had been removed, there was no promise of a clean bill of health. We remained optimistic as he had bounced back so beautifully and decided to enjoy every precious moment, envisioning that time was on our side.

He continued to delight his audiences with his singing, hiding the draining tube from the operation in a bag inside his jacket. Nothing was going to stop him performing and, being the great showman that he was, he convinced his fans that he was getting better. If only that could have been the case, but sadly all was not well, and it wasn't very long before his symptoms escalated.

One balmy Autumn Queensland morning we decided to drop everything and drive to our favourite eating place at Tumbulgum. We sat across from the sparkling water, and everything seemed super clear. Holding hands across the table, we felt so grateful for the special years we had enjoyed together and believed that we could conquer the world. We vowed to make the most of every precious moment. I will always be grateful for that memory as only an hour later we were confronted by the next stage of Mick's illness. Back at home, still wrapped in a cloak of contentment, I was working at my desk and could hear Mick singing away as he arranged CDs that he intended to play on the FM Jazz radio he hosted on Monday evenings. The sun was streaming in the window, sending shadows dancing around the walls. Birds were fluttering in the trees outside, their songs filling the stillness. My heart swelled with gratitude.

A piercing scream, followed by an ominous thud, jolted me out of my reverie. I raced upstairs to find my beautiful, previously fit, husband writhing on the floor in a seizure. I did what I could to turn him on his side and rang 000. A friendly voice on the other end kept talking to me while we waited for an ambulance. My darling didn't stir as I held him tightly in an embrace. I remember begging him not to die. I couldn't conceive a life without him.

The news delivered to us that night was not good. A tumour had been located in the middle, most inaccessible part of his brain. Mick maintained his brave face and asked to have it cut out as soon as possible so he could start recovering and be well enough to attend a major gig he had been booked to perform in.

The next few months were a nightmare. The week after his seizure, I travelled every day to the hospital and put on a brave face as we waited for the prognosis from specialists who would decide if surgery was going to be an option. Always the essence of positivity, he entertained the other occupants of the four-bed ward he was assigned to with anecdotes and encouraged them to make more of an effort to get well. It was heartbreaking, and each day on the drive home I would have tears running down my cheeks.

The morning arrived when the brain specialist took me aside and gave me the news I had been dreading. The team had decided not to operate as the risk that he would become paralysed and without a voice was quite high. This was not a life Mick would choose for himself, so our hopes for recovery were dashed. The doctor advised me to take him home and give him a good life.

In the hospital, he had been his normal loving self, but returning home he seemed to become two different people. When any of his friends or family were around, particularly his musician friends, he would be charming and totally normal, but when they were gone, my previously loving husband was a different person. His behaviour was sometimes quite bizarre, but only around me. This caused a dissidence in the way I was perceived. When attempting to convey to others how ill he was, I was simply not believed.

It was a lonely time made more devastating by Mick's changed behaviour. This man whom I adored, whilst being totally reliant on me, was often quite dismissive. I would remind myself often that it was the effect of the tumour. Eventually, it caught up with us when he began making some bizarre decisions. By this stage, I had become rather worn down, but as I wanted so much to please him, I would try to go along with his requests, often against my better judgement. To be honest, I wasn't thinking about what might happen when the time came for me to be alone, I just wanted Mick to be happy and be the man I had loved these past years.

Whilst I was battling to keep on top of things, there were some memorable experiences. Mick's music kept some part of him alive and only weeks before he died, he gave the performance of a lifetime to a large audience of ardent fans. He didn't miss a beat, and I believe he was given the added strength that day to help him perform at his stunning best. Radium had melted all of his hair, and his usually taut belly was swollen by steroids, but to those of us who loved him, he was the most beautiful sight and sound. I had asked if he would please sing the song he often sang for me at gigs. He told me he would certainly do this for me, but on the night he forgot, and I was devastated. He did call me up on stage and pushed a microphone in front of me not realising that, for some reason, I had completely lost my voice. Having no voice had its benefits as it precluded me from answering endless questions from the huge crowd, but was not useful when my husband wanted me to join him in a song on stage. The song wasn't even one of my favourites. I was longing for a last rendition of "*Wild Thing, you make my heart sing.*" This was the song our hearts had sung in unison for so many years.

A few weeks after Mick's death, I happened to be looking at YouTube clips and found that several weeks before his death he had posted a clip taken a few months earlier when he sang *Wild Thing* at a fiftieth birthday party. He had written an inscription under the clip that read:

"This is for my beautiful wife who will always be my wild thing." He hadn't forgotten after all.

His last performance had sucked the last bit of his strength, and his further decline was rapid. It wasn't long after that I had to face the fact that I could not manage him on my own. He refused to eat or drink and once more he was taken by ambulance to the hospital. Sadly, this time there was no turning back. Other tumours had formed, and he was placed into palliative care.

There happened to be one room vacant, and it proved to be a beautiful place for him. The large windows looked out to a spectacular view of mountains and trees and, apart from the medical equipment, it could have passed as a rather luxurious hotel room. Sadly, he was past the point of really being able to appreciate his surroundings. The care he received was more than I could have hoped for. He was content to lie still and declined my offer to provide him with music, television or even a radio which he had always loved. I would crawl into bed with him, and for short periods, when he was lucid, we were able to recapture the special love we had shared. I would remind him of the first time we met and how he hadn't told me that he was an accomplished musician. I fell in love with this quiet English gentleman completely unaware of the shock awaiting me. Three weeks after we met, he asked me to marry him. I was stunned. It was not what I was expecting. I was even more stunned when he asked if I was interested in coming with him to the Jazz Club to watch him perform.

On the way to the club, he mentioned that he wasn't the best Jazz singer in the world and I secretly hoped this was not going to be embarrassing. Little did I know I was about to be confronted by the biggest shock of all. My quiet English gentleman turned into a hurricane on stage. He was magnificent, and it was then I learned that he had been the lead singer for *The Purple Hearts*, my favourite band of the sixties. Never did I imagine myself walking down the aisle to my hero singing *Wild Thing, You Make My Heart Sing.* And oh, how I did make his heart sing, as he did mine. It then became our signature song. Until his illness, we experienced something quite magical. I would find little notes and poems left in all sorts of places and whilst he was often surrounded by adoring women at his gigs, I was never concerned as I always knew that I was the 'Wild Thing' he came back to every night. Lying together in his bed in palliative care, he liked to hear me speak of these times and was very much at peace.

I've always believed in speaking honestly with those who are facing the end of this life. I had not been close to my mother but, at the end of her life, she turned to me because she knew we could have open conversations about what she was about to face. She even had me purchase special burial clothes for her. When I presented them to her to make sure they were what she wanted, certain members of the family expressed that they found this quite macabre.

As a young woman, I had a near death experience following surgery which resulted in a severe case of septicaemia. I was extremely ill, but the experience was enough to assure me that death is not at all the terrible fate that it is sometimes painted to be. It was not my time, but I was not at all anxious to come back. The memory of this helped me to have no qualms about sharing honest conversations about death with Mick if that is what he wanted. He was grateful for this and never showed one bit of regret or fear. We even had some laughter when something funny would occur. I arrived at his bedside with a photo cut from the local newspaper one morning. It announced the death of the talented African American musician known as Wiley Reid. Mick immediately knew who he was.

"Bloody Wiley Reid, I gave a benefit concert for him fifteen years ago because he was supposed to cark it, and he's still beaten me to it." He laughed and then remarked that this black face kept appearing to him and we joked that it was just Wiley telling him to hurry up and join the band. It was lovely to hear his laughter and his acceptance of what was happening to him.

One morning when I lay snuggled beside Mick, he turned to me and said, "I want to go, darling." Another moment I had dreaded had come, but I knew what I had to do. Swallowing hard and hugging him tightly, I said,

"My darling, this has to be your choice. I know you don't want to be here if you can't sing. I am going to miss you so much, but I respect your wishes." I was unprepared for how grateful he was.

"Thank you so much, darling." Mick became quite animated as he spoke of how he would be able to see people he had lost so long ago. With these last words, he dropped into a peaceful sleep. I still have a photo of the beautiful smile he had on his lips.

The next morning a close friend visited Mick in hospital. They enjoyed a robust chat about days long past. As he was about to leave, his friend touched Mick's shoulder and said, "Hang in there, mate." I saw Mick shudder and his whole demeanour change. When I asked him what was wrong he said, "Does that mean that I can't go?" Then I realised what had been troubling him. Well-meaning people would try to encourage him by telling him that he was going to be fine or something similar. It is a very natural thing for people to say. Always wanting to please, he hated letting anybody down, even in these circumstances. I hastened to assure him that it was all okay.

"Who loves you more than anyone else in all the whole world?" I asked him.

"You," he answered.

"Didn't we agree that this has to be your choice and I would support you in that choice?" I reminded him. His face cleared once more, and he thanked me profusely.

A few days before Mick died, I had been scheduled to give a talk to a group of business women in Brisbane. The night before the talk I couldn't find my laptop which contained my powerpoint slides. I was unreasonably distraught and apparently called my daughter a number of times. The only thing I can remember is her saying that maybe I didn't need the slides and why didn't I just speak from the heart. I stood by the window in the kitchen sobbing loudly. How could I speak from my heart when it was breaking into little pieces? This was my lowest point. I heard myself repeatedly saying, "I can't bear it, I can't bear it." Through the fog of my tears, I heard a voice say, "Well you just have to bear it. You can do this." I prepared myself a hot bath and added some precious drops of lavender. As I soaked into the fragrant heat, reason returned, and I knew the voice was right. I just had to bear it. I could do this.

Thanks to my daughter's wisdom, I have never used PowerPoint slides again and much prefer to gauge the audience and speak from the heart. That day, I gave my presentation straight from my heart as my husband spent his last few days on this earth. It was an unusually sacred experience. At the beginning of my talk, nobody knew that my husband was dying, and I didn't say anything until the last minute. I felt quite composed and found the audience very receptive, so I decided to share my husband's plight with them. It was at that moment when tears began to slide down my face, and my grief was shared as others began dabbing their eyes in empathy. There were twenty-five special women in attendance that morning, and I sold twenty-eight copies of my book, *Sizzling at Seventy – Victim to Victorious*. Mick had been such a great supporter of my book and would have been thrilled at this result, but sadly at this stage, he was past showing enthusiasm about such mundane things as book sales.

I would like to believe that I helped Mick in his final days to be very peaceful. I didn't want him to be aware of any turmoil that may be happening around him. One evening, as I readied myself for bed, the hospital called and said I should come as there had been a change. I regret that I stopped to get dressed. When I arrived at the hospital, he had been gone only five minutes. Maybe that is what he wanted. It all felt so surreal. The nurses had dressed him in his favourite shirt and placed a white rose on his chest. He looked so peaceful it was hard to believe that he was really gone. I felt his presence so keenly and never have I loved him more.

Losing my beloved was the hardest thing I have experienced, yet today I can say that he gave me the gift of grief. Not being particularly close to my parents, I had never lost anyone that I so dearly loved before. There is much that I have learnt from this experience, one lesson being that we all grieve differently. It is so important to communicate with all loved ones in the language that they understand. I made the mistake of thinking that his family and friends all understood what was happening to him and was unprepared for the outcomes of the lack of constructive communication about what steps needed to be taken.

Sarah Kerr pinned down what often happens when we are facing the death of a beloved. She says that it takes a while for our souls to accept the inevitability of what is about to happen. She has witnessed a series of steps that people can go through – a model from Family Systems Constellation. The steps are Acknowledge, Accept and Agree. At the beginning some people don't want to acknowledge what is happening – they just don't want it to be true. They don't talk about it so they won't let it come into their space. The next stage is acknowledging but not accepting. They will say they hate what is happening. They know it is happening, but they are still fighting against it. The third stage is agreement - which Sarah explains as, 'The unconditional co-operation with the unavoidable. We don't want what's coming, we don't want it to be coming, but we know it is coming. Instead of denying, we say, "This is where we are going. How do we do it as well as we can." If we can come to an agreement with death, we can meet it with much more grace and confidence.' I wish I had understood these steps as I blindly attempted to navigate an unchartered path. Some of those who had been close to Mick were stuck in the first two stages and I didn't realise. How different everything would have been if we all could have reached that third stage together.

One particularly sad consequence of this affected me deeply. Two days after Mick's death, a friend called me and told me that he had seen the notification about Mick's cremation on Facebook. I assured him that couldn't be so as I had believed that I would be included in the planning and process of his burial, but somehow there had been some miscommunication and the cremation of my husband had indeed taken place. If I had been in my right mind, this would not have happened, but there was now nothing I could do.

The telephone constantly rang with requests from many of Mick's fans, who wanted to attend his funeral. I explained that he hadn't wanted a funeral but that hopefully there would be some celebration of his life.

By this time my behaviour had become quite erratic, and I don't remember a great deal, but unfortunately some of the emails I sent upset members of the family. I really can't remember what I wrote. My main aim was to keep the family informed, but now I understand the three stages we can experience when a loved one is facing death, I realise that my attempts to keep them up to date were perceived as me making trouble. There was never any ill intent on my part, but I would certainly counsel others experiencing grief to shut down the computer and keep it shut.

There was one more important task for me to fulfil before I could allow myself to cave in completely. With so many requests from those who wished to have the opportunity to pay their respects to this man who had provided so much pleasure for so many years, I decided to organise a fitting musical tribute to Mick. With the help of a couple of his band members, we managed to track down all surviving musicians who had ever played with him. The number was quite significant, and all those invited were keen to take part. I visited a number of hotels where Mick had played over the years and found *The Jubilee* to be very receptive to allowing access to all facilities for the hours between 4.00pm and 11.00pm.

It was a fabulous night, and I felt Mick's presence as we celebrated his memory and amazing talent. A pivotal moment was the last song, 'Let the good times roll.' On a large screen at the back of the stage, we could see a projection of Mick singing his heart out with this final rendition of his favourite song that he had sung at his very last gig. I'm sure he would have loved seeing everyone dancing and singing along. I had thought about releasing some doves into the sky at the end of the night, but it was too late in the evening for little doves, so we had to be content to say our goodbyes by releasing balloons as a tribute, which for the sake of the environment, we later retrieved.

Once Mick's spectacular tribute was over, I fell in a heap. My friends and family didn't know what to do with me, and neither did I, but now I know that most of all I needed a hug. I learnt that is what most people need when they are suffering from grief, or if they are not hugging types, just a reassuring pat on the arm. What they don't need is advice or platitudes. Brené Brown's statement that any sentence that begins with "At least…" is not coming from a person who understands about empathy. I did get some 'At leasts' - "*At least you had those good years together!*" "*At least he didn't suffer…*" I shudder when I think that maybe there had been a time when I threw out a few such platitudes. We all want to make people feel better and sometimes it is hard to know what to say. I have learnt that to say nothing is better than something patronising, but please don't ignore a grieving person as if they have the plague. A hug is going to be more reassuring than anything you can say.

My friend Tony turned up unexpectedly one evening and found me prostrate on the floor. He picked me up and hugged me so tight it released the tears that had welled up inside me.

He held me until they were completely spent. I was fortunate to have a few loyal friends who put up with my incessant chatter. It was almost as if I needed to fill up any empty spaces with words. I spent a great deal of time on my own, but when someone was with me, the words tumbled out. I don't remember much about this but have been reminded by a few friends who had witnessed my distress.

One of my favourite memories with Mick was in a huge old cathedral in London where we sat together and listened to a beautiful rendition, with harp and cello, of Saint Saens magnificent piece, *The Swan*. We both sat with the tears streaming down our faces. It was to this piece I turned in my hours of deepest grief. All night this piece of music and a few others played repeatedly as I lay on the couch where Mick and I had spent many unforgettable hours listening to music, watching special shows and often debating about issues that interested us. Always we sat holding hands or with arms loosely around each other. We loved our time together.

How each person reacts to grief is unpredictable, and sometimes the reaction of others can be challenging. Knowing what I understand now, I would do some things differently. As I mentioned before, one thing I would certainly counsel others to do is close down their computer and restrain themselves from sending emails whilst their emotions are still raw. Emails sent when emotions are high can be misinterpreted and can cause huge disharmony.

My grandchildren have been known to say, "Remember the time before you went nuts Mema…" I unknowingly created a new timeline for them a 'Pre-nuts,' and 'Post-nuts' period. Frustratingly, the post-nuts period lasted for much longer than I had anticipated. I apparently made $4,000 worth of phone calls that I have no memory of making. Bills came in from everywhere, and with my current state of limited income I had no idea how I was going to manage, but miraculously I did, by paying little bits at a time.

It was a few months later that I found myself conversing with the statue of Mahatma. I'm sure passers-by would have found this a strange sight. Fortunately, I wasn't taken away by men in white coats to be mentally assessed. As I sat on my favourite park bench, I began to reflect on how hard I had been trying to get well with absolutely no improvement. Along with my daily meditations I had diligently worked with the "28 days of gratitude" program from Rhonda Byrnes book *Magic* and Brenda Davies-*The 7 Healing Chakras Workbook – Exercises and meditations for unlocking your body's energy centres.* There was also other ponderous reading material that didn't seem to do the trick either. I would now encourage others suffering a deep state of grief to be more gentle with themselves. These activities were possibly a bit demanding for someone in my fragile state of mind. It didn't help that I expected so much more of myself and began to lose confidence in my ability to heal. Earlier in my life, I had overcome some serious illnesses, but I now understand, that grief is the hardest one of all to heal. Having come out the other end, I feel I now have the skills to assist others going through these experiences.

I remember thinking that all of this heavy stuff had done me no good and decided that I would just go and buy a trashy magazine to read. I will never know what made me choose a magazine that I would never normally pick up, except maybe in a dental surgery. I went back to Mahatma and began flicking listlessly through the pages. What I am going to recount may sound extremely fatuous, but it was my experience. These headlines appeared on the page, *"When you are grieving, look for signs that you are being taken care of."* These were words written by a well-known psychic medium, and his counsel was that I must look for lots of butterflies, foreign money appearing unexpectedly and white feathers. I shut the magazine scornfully and suddenly noticed dozens of colourful butterflies all around me. They were so beautiful, and I just wondered why I hadn't noticed them before. I trudged back to my son's home, and as I walked into my bedroom, I noticed a Euro currency note on the floor. My son had been to a conference in Finland, but the note certainly hadn't been visible in the room before, and there was no other person in the house. I sat on the side of the bed and thought of all the possibilities of how the foreign note had come to be there, but finally decided that it must have blown there from somewhere. For some reason I found myself walking towards the front door and was stunned to see dozens of white feathers all over the front lawn. This set me back in my tracks, but I just put it down to the yellow car syndrome – when you buy a yellow car, you see yellow cars everywhere.

I dismissed the whole matter until I sat down at my computer. My son had set it up for me in a little room which only contained a desk and chair. I was attempting to finish a task I had started sometime before, and as I typed away, I saw something fall from the ceiling past my eyes and land on the floor. My heart skipped a beat when I saw that it was a Malaysian twenty cent piece. There was nowhere that it could have fallen from and no matter how hard I tried for an explanation, there simply was none. "Okay, I get it - whatever force is trying to convince me, I am convinced." At that moment, I knew I was going to get well. Since that incident, I have had many wonderful affirmations and have my own explanation regarding this phenomenon, which does not satisfy sceptics. However, everyone was relieved when they could see there was a shift in me. It didn't happen overnight, but I knew at that time I was on the road to regaining my mental health.

The first thing that needed to happen was for me to learn to love myself. How could I expect others to love and understand me if I couldn't accept and love the person that I was at that time? I had written affirmations every day in the 28-day gratitude program, but I had made it a rather mechanical exercise. My friend says that affirmations can be just like jam on mouldy bread and at that time that is all they really were. I am glad to say the mouldy bread is gone and I now spread my affirmations on fresh, yummy bread made of self-love. All I could think about after Mick had passed, was how I could have done things differently. Did I do everything I could to care for my much-loved husband?

Everybody experiences grief at some time in their lives. Whilst we commonly look at death being the most common cause of our grief, there are so many more of life's challenges that can cause us to grieve. This book includes case studies from people I have interviewed who have suffered grief for a number of reasons. These include the loss of a loved one, the loss of a marriage through divorce, the loss of beloved pets, the loss of a son's mobility, loss of identity, the loss of dignity. In fact, grief can be encapsulated by stating that when we lose anything that has meaning for us, we will experience grief.

There are so many factors that can cause a person to grieve and whatever the cause, it is vital that we understand that whilst everyone handles their grief in different ways and with individual intensity and duration, the grief experience will affect so many aspects of our being. Life is never quite the same. I love this quote from Elizabeth Kubler Ross.

> *The most beautiful people we have known are those who have known defeat, known suffering, known struggle, known loss, and have found their way out of those depths. People are like stained - glass windows. They sparkle and shine when the sun is out, but when the darkness sets in, their true beauty is revealed, only if there is a light within.*

In this book, people have so generously shared their experiences, and in each case, they have found that it is possible that each experience has led them to function at a higher level. Helen Keller was someone who had much to grieve following the loss of her sight and hearing at the age of two, yet she went on to achieve great things. This profound quote from Helen, "*Although the world is full of sorrow, it is full also of the overcoming of it.*"

I recall a time when I was sitting on a bench in the supermarket, waiting for my daughter-in-law, when the lady sitting next to me struck up a conversation. It didn't take long to realise that this was a practice she followed almost every day in the hope that someone would engage with her. She told me that her husband had passed away suddenly six years ago, and her friends were tired of her because she just couldn't get over it. Getting over it is a notion that I would like to see banished. Grief is not a linear process, and I don't even think of it as being circular. Whilst time can help, that doesn't mean that waves of sadness cannot envelop us forever, often when we least expect it. I have had clients who have berated themselves for not 'getting over it'. Whilst I agree that there are stages of a grief process we are likely to go through, the inevitable ending is not that our sadness is over forever, but as time passes, the episodes of deep sadness tend to be further apart, and we can allow joy to find its way into our hearts.

In my previous book, *Sizzling at Seventy – Victim to Victorious*, I explained how the understanding I now have about moods and emotions has helped me to make important distinctions between a mood and an emotion. Moods last longer and remain in the background of our lives influencing the way we live and act. We are not always aware that a particular mood may be linked to a particular event. Emotions are different in that they may be triggered by an event. When we grieve, we yearn for someone or some situation that is now lost to us.

It is completely normal for us to find difficulty in accepting the loss and even feeling that life is not worth living. This mood can be accompanied by a myriad of emotions such as guilt. You may question yourself as to whether you did enough in a given situation or question what you could have done differently. Another emotion is anger. This can be for a number of reasons such as feeling that you've been left with a terrible mess, especially if financial affairs or documents were not in order. These are some examples of emotions that can keep us trapped with our loss and in denial.

Although there is much pain involved, there can be a kind of beauty and dignity about death, particularly when we can share the process with our loved ones. We are all going to die and I was overwhelmed by the gratitude and love I felt while experiencing Mick's passing. I have always been one to look for the light at the end of the tunnel and then blast my way through towards it. Sometimes this is not possible as there is so much for us to learn and experience along the journey. There is always a gift at the end of it, and we need to take whatever time we need to be able to receive that gift.

1. LYN'S HEALING TOOLBOX

Grief comes in all forms. Before we lose someone, there is often a great deal of grief involved. Upon reflection, I might have done things differently. Here are some tips that I wish I had been given when I was stumbling through on my own.

- Make a list of things you need to prepare for. I think I may have been in denial and being more prepared would have saved so much heartache later.
- Be aware of the three steps outlined by Sarah Kerr: Acknowledge, Accept, Agree. There are more details in the reference section at the end of this book.
- Make an effort to communicate effectively with all stakeholders, even when you know it might be difficult. Every person involved needs to clearly understand any process that is undertaken.
- Phone or arrange a meeting rather than sending emails as they can sometimes be misinterpreted.
- This is not a time to be trying to please others. Take care of yourself and do what is best for you. I almost gave away the house I worked so hard for in my desire to help others heal and my efforts were misinterpreted. Do what is best for you and your loved one.
- There will always be people who will want to offer advice. Follow your own intuition.
- If people ask if they can do something be sure and ask for a hug. Hugs are always important. Food is okay too!
- Love and nurture yourself. You are doing the best you can.
- Try and retain open communication with your loved one. In my experience, I have found it beneficial to talk openly about what is about to happen and find out anything they might like you to do. This was difficult in my case as Mick's brain tumour had him coming up with ideas when his brain was scrambled, but there were days when he was lucid.
- My experience was also that Mick was happy to talk about his impending passing and when he felt the time was near, he was

very peaceful. I do not believe it is helpful to reassure the dying that they are going to get better. They sometimes need our permission to leave.

- Know that you are never alone. I lost sight of this and struggled to get it back. A daily practice such as meditation or journaling can be helpful.

CHAPTER 2

Searching For
The Next Steps

This book began with the notion that it would be about grief in its many forms. As it progressed, I was given the message to go one step further past the many forms of grief and its stages to where we can find our fabulous again, or maybe even for the first time. Being fabulous is not an end in itself as life is a never-ending journey.

On my return from my stay in Canberra, I was determined to get on top of my game. However, my transformation certainly didn't happen overnight. The most important thing I had to address was saving my home. I had been in such a strange state I almost gave my home away. Had it not been for those good souls that cautioned me to wait a year before I made any decisions, I may have found myself living in a box. When we are experiencing extreme grief, we tend to want to do anything to take the pain away, but there are no shortcuts. I had felt that if I did some good stuff for the people who in their own grief had hurt me deeply, I would be able to make things right between us. It would have been to my own detriment, and I now know it would not have won me any favours or understanding. I am willing to see my part in the breakdowns that occurred. Sometimes we just have to let everything play out.

Things started to look up when I stopped looking to others for answers and took up the reins of how I wanted to live my life moving forward. I didn't just want to survive, I wanted to regain my life and find a new purpose. I was faced with a decision to either focus on the pain and create a story about that, or look at a more positive narrative of what I wanted my future to be? It was a no-brainer to choose the latter. I had promised Mick that I would continue to write and speak where possible. He had been such an inspiration in my life and believed I could do anything.

My next priority was to get myself out of the debts that had accumulated in the past year which were far more than I had realised. Fortunately, I was able to secure enough work projects to keep me solvent and avert my desire to want to escape to a cave. Magical things begin to happen when we change our thinking and trust the process. Unexpected gifts can come to us when we least expect them as was the case for me when Mick's band members so generously donated much-needed funds.

At the beginning of each year I always do a vision board and even though I was not in the best mental state of mind that January, I managed to write down all I desired for the year. One of my wishes was that Hay House would recognise my book, *Sizzling at Seventy – Victim to Victorious*. For some unknown reason, I didn't use the word 'publish' but used the word 'recognise'. Six months later, an unexpected phone call jolted me out of some apathy. It was Leon Nascon from Hay House.

"Lyn, we love your book and want to give you some publicity," He announced. I was gobsmacked and yet I shouldn't have been. After all, I had written on my vision board that I wanted Hay House to recognise my book.

What followed were a number of radio interviews, which I quite enjoyed. Some of them were fun and were kept a bit lighter than others. One interviewer wanted to pair me off with his 80-year-old father. This was after telling me about his father's illnesses and how difficult he was. Did he think I was already desperate and dateless? I graciously declined his offer. It was a relief to enjoy this lightness and be able to laugh. In contrast, the next interview was particularly gruelling as questions were put to me that were difficult to answer.

One particular interviewer had known Mick and his work, which made our discourse quite emotional. He had read *Sizzling at Seventy* and asked me how I felt about my mother now. I said that although I had hated her when she died, I had since gained love and appreciation for her. His response amazed me.

"How can you possibly love her. She wrecked your life?" He seemed quite angry. I explained to him that having experienced my rebirthing, I had gained insights into why I chose her to be my mother and now understood that she was only acting out of her own wounded space. Regardless of the pain, I went through, I now understand that this was part of my journey. She taught me so much, and I am a much stronger woman because of all that happened between us.

It is fascinating to look back and review my life and how the painful experiences fit into the whole journey. Here I was in deep grief, undertaking interviews about a book I had written while Mick was alive, and although it made me appreciate where I had come from, nobody would let me talk about what had been happening since his death. This caused me to feel alienated. I allowed people to tell me what I should be doing and how I should be feeling. I was given loads of advice such as: *"Let it go." "Don't talk about it."* The truth is that it isn't quite as simple as that and I think if I'd had the chance to talk it out, I would have made sense of it all a lot quicker. However, I am glad that the people who love me didn't want me to fall into victimhood again and this was their way of showing me love. I understand that now.

It is hard to pinpoint the moment when I woke up one day and knew that I had crawled out of the dark hole and was ready to face the world again. I began to use the strategies that I had written so passionately about in my previous book and found that they worked. I treasure my mood framework and whilst I leant heavily on it in my last book, I will refer to it again now. I forced myself to observe the moods I was operating out of and was able to gradually shift my resentment to acceptance. I couldn't change what had happened, but I could take some actions to move forward. I recognised the resignation I was steeped in – the hidden 'but' hanging in the very air I breathed. I wanted to change things, 'but' I didn't know how. I began to feel the seed of hope and ambition germinating. Then there was that old mood of anxiety causing me to breathe in shallow bursts, and I reached deep into my memory to recapture the mood of wonder that had been so much part of my life before all of this happened. Gradually, I felt ready to face the world again. This is what my mood framework looked like:

DECLARATION	FACTICITY – Facts that we assess as unchangeable	POSSIBILITY- What we assess as changeable	UNCERTAINTY- What we cannot confidently predict
The mood of Opposition	Why were these awful things happening to me? I didn't deserve it. This caused me to have a mood of **Resentment** which wasn't getting me anywhere and *stopped me from getting past it.*	I wanted to change things, **but** I didn't think I was capable. I wasn't good enough. I didn't know where to start. I was in the mood of **Resignation**. I had to change my language: *I can't do this. It's never going to be any better.*	I don't know what is going to happen. I could lose my house. I have no idea what the future holds for me. I was now in the moods of **Anxiety** and **Fear**. *I was feeling confused and threatened.*
The mood of Acceptance	Making up my mind that I wanted to focus on the bigger narrative helped me to get into the mood of **Acceptance**. *I couldn't change it, but I had come to terms with what had happened and chose to move on.* Not from my sadness but from the resentment.	I will give it a go – I have nothing to lose. I can do this. I'll put on a tribute concert for Mick. This will lead me to the next step and will be a great legacy for him. It will give me something positive to do. Now I was in the mood of **Ambition** and saying, "Let's go for it."	It was such a relief for me when I faced that even though I couldn't know exactly what was ahead of me, I could start putting things in place, and I went into the beautiful mood of **Wonder**. *I was ready to explore and experiment.*

I miss my Mick terribly and still hold in-depth conversations with him. It's a comfort to know he believed in me and wanted me to continue with the work we started together.

I had relished his musical successes. My heart would burst with pride every time I watched him on stage, particularly when he sang the blues. He would pour so much feeling into those old blues songs. Understandably, he had been labelled, "*Just a white boy singing the blues*". Many loved his rock 'n roll music because he inspired them to let their hair down and dance until they dropped, but it was when he sang the blues my heart would swell, and tears would run down my face. These are the memories that soothe my pain.

2. LYN'S HEALING TOOLBOX

Everyone will have a different experience. Here is what I have learnt from my grief.

- Be gentle with yourself. Take each day as it comes. You may find yourself feeling strange and acting differently. Just observe – don't judge. This will pass when you are ready. Trusting that you will feel better really helps get through the process.
- It is **vital** that you don't make any big decisions or take any actions for **at least a year**.
- There is no time frame.
- Sadly, death can bring out some unusual behaviours – everyone grieves differently. Try not to take things personally.
- There will always be people who will want to offer advice. Follow your own intuition.
- Exercise in some form is very healing. You may not feel like eating but make sure you get enough nutrition in some form. I found shakes were good.
- Love and nurture yourself. You have done the best that you could.
- Feel free to talk about your loved one. Find someone you can trust and who will allow you to talk, even if it is a counsellor.
- Make your own mood framework and put it on the fridge. Check in each day and if you find yourself continually in the negative moods, take action. Also, watch your breathing. You will find that if you are in the top three moods, your breathing will be shallow. Practice deep breathing and good posture.
- Remind yourself often that whilst there is no time frame on grieving, you will begin to feel better. Just believing this helped me through some rough times.

CHAPTER 3

How I Inherited My Ex-husband's Wife

As I get older, I am so grateful for the strange twists and turns in my life. We cannot always predict them, but we can choose to embrace them as there is always a positive lesson to learn. As I began to recover from the worst of my grief, I encountered a 'twist' that I certainly could not have predicted. Who would dream that they could inherit their ex-husband's wife? Yes, you read it right because that is what happened.

I have watched some of my friends take on the responsibility of caring for their ageing parents, and I often felt grateful that I had missed that painful sojourn. However, my smugness was short lived as another character-building exercise presented itself to me. I was able to witness someone grieving which had tragic consequences.

The father of my children was ten years older than me, and when we divorced over thirty years ago, he met Pat who was five years older than him, making her fifteen years my senior. She was financially well off which enabled him to live a life of ease, although he contributed nothing to our three children or me. I have often been grateful as it forced me to find resources that have enhanced my ability to work and keep active.

For some reason, right from the beginning, Pat was keen to have me as a friend, even though we had absolutely nothing in common.

She told me several years after we had met that she had initially hated me. Before our first meeting, John had not prepared her for my comparative youth and what she assessed as good looks. She was quite hostile towards me when we first met, but on a subsequent meeting she apologised for her frostiness and we would occasionally meet up for family occasions.

As the years progressed, my ex-husband began to weaken and he became seriously ill. Pat also lost a great deal of her strength and was subjected to a number of back operations which didn't always go according to plan and left her with a much-reduced mobility. It was at this time she called on me more and more and when John was in full-time care, I would take her to see him, often in a wheelchair. When he passed away in 2011, I thought that the thread of our relationship would unravel as I became tied up with nursing my own ill husband, but she hung in there.

Now here comes the important part that reminds us how vulnerable the elderly can be and how greed can allow some humans to concoct insidious schemes at the expense of another person's safety.

Twenty-five years ago, Pat and my ex-husband bought a villa in a retirement village located in a pretty town in northern New South Wales. Their villa was built on a lakeside. As they enjoyed a cuppa on their deck, they would bask in the beauty of the sparkling lake with its unique bird life. Graceful black swans would glide by, often with little cygnets trailing behind. Pelicans would dive down to swoop up a fish in their beaks and transfer it into their large throat pouches. Water hens would dart in and out of the bull rushes and little brown ducks with shiny blue feathers would swim lazily around, occasionally dipping down to catch their meal of smaller fish. Pat and John loved the vast wildlife, particularly the water dragons that would creep to the deck, thankfully swallow a proffered grape, and scuttle back to the water. Their villa was quite spacious with two large bedrooms, two large living areas, a kitchen and two bathrooms, one of which contained a luxurious spa bath. The added bonus was the spectacular deck overlooking the lake. Pat was very good at creating a comfortable home and an exquisite garden. In some ways, they lived an idyllic life, until John's health began to deteriorate.

Whilst complaints and irritability were a hallmark of her personality, Pat thrived on being needed, and our family was thankful that she relished her task as John's nurse. It would have been difficult for any one of us to take care of him. John and Pat shared many values that were so different from mine. I sometimes found it distressing and had to draw the line on their frequent irreverent jokes levelled at causes I held sacred, particularly when it came to marginalised minority groups, the Indigenous, refugees, the LGBT groups and others. It wasn't hard to see why my marriage to John had not been sustainable. However, he was still the father of my children, and I will always honour him for that. I am glad I was able to thank him for our three special children before he died.

Pat was very lonely after John's death. This made her a vulnerable target for a handyman who worked around the village. He gave her a convincing sob story of how he had been done over by two women and now was struggling to make ends meet. Pat was immediately drawn into his story. She had always liked having younger men around and whilst no one else believed in him, she felt that it might be mutually advantageous for him to live in her spare room and do odd jobs for her in lieu of rent. She proudly told me that, as he was only fifty-three years old, she had a 'toy boy'. As far as I know, there wasn't any physical element to the relationship. However, as she was very nervous about being on her own at night, she enjoyed having a man in the house. He did not pay any rent but cooked her evening meal and did her shopping. She had hoped that he would do other chores in the house and garden, but as the months went by, he did less and less.

Along with her friends in the village, I was very suspicious of this arrangement, but she kept assuring me that he was good to her. She seemed so happy at first, hence I didn't feel it was my place to interfere. However, I became very concerned when she told me that because everyone in the village hated him, he wanted her to sell up and move into a rental property to get away from these nasty people. He succeeded in alienating her from all her village contacts.

I kept hoping that I might be wrong about my misgivings and whilst she was happy about the arrangement, it was none of my business. He became her registered carer, and she became more and more dependent on him. In the early days of their arrangement, he treated her reasonably well and I did not see her very often. After about two years she began calling on me again and I was shocked to find him speaking very roughly to her. He had talked her into selling her car and buying a better car for him to drive her around. An impressive four-wheel drive vehicle was purchased, but the promised outings never eventuated. He would take her to doctor's visits and places where he could be seen to be the hands-on carer, going as far as telling people he was her son. As for the longed-for trips together, they never eventuated.

Pat's main passion in life was her dog, Timmy. They shared a rather unique and special partnership. He was getting old but still had youthful vigour and absolute devotion to his mistress. They hated being apart, so when Pat broke her hip in that second year and was admitted to the hospital, she was grateful that her carer would be there to comfort her faithful companion. This is where the story becomes particularly eerie, and the moment when I suspected that I would need to intervene.

She was distraught when told that her beloved pet had died the day after her admission to hospital. The tale this charlatan told her was that a neighbour had thrown Timmy in the lake beside the house. His tale was that he had arrived home from work to find the little dog floating in deep water. With great valour, he had stripped off and plunged into the icy cold lake in an attempt to save the dog, but alas it was too late. So, he had taken him over to the golf club and buried him. When I heard this obviously ridiculous story, I knew that my instincts had been correct, but she was still bewitched by him and believed everything he said.

Maybe if he had continued to be caring and looking after her needs, he might have been able to get away with what was obviously a well-crafted plot to feather his nest, but he made a couple of slip-ups. He had been telling her for over a year that she was 'losing it' and even hiding things so she would think she really was in fact, losing her mind. I cannot prove it, but I suspect he may have been interfering with her medication as she often complained of dizziness and an inability to remember things. We now know that he planned to get a medical certificate which would deem her incompetent. It was his impatience to have this happen that began to raise some question's in Pat's mind, and she became more fearful.

A week after her dismissal from the hospital, she called me and begged me to come to her as soon as possible. She told me that she felt afraid and had to get away. While she had been in the hospital, we discussed the idea of her moving to a facility that would provide more care. I suggested taking a look at a particular place that she had mentioned.

When I arrived to pick her up, I could see that her 'carer' was quite agitated and told me that she was really losing it. When he informed me that he was taking her to his doctor the next day to verify that she was incapable of looking after herself, alarm bells rang for me. He complained to me that he had been looking after for a few years without any thanks from anybody. I told him that I was taking Pat for a drive.

As we drove to the facility that had taken her interest, she told me some stories that certainly affirmed all of my fears. I felt sad when she lifted her little-wizened face to mine and said that he wouldn't even hug her anymore.

She looked so frail and quite vague as I wheeled her around the facility she had chosen to see. Later I realised that she wasn't really aware of what was happening, but she agreed that she would be safe there. As the manager gave us a tour of the facility, I told her Pat's story, expressing my concerns. It made me shudder when she said that it was not uncommon for the elderly to be taken advantage of in this way.

Pat chose a unit that she felt she would like to purchase, deciding that she was ready to sell her lovely place on the lake and move into a facility which could provide her with the care she required at this stage in her life.

This was the beginning of a life-changing event for me. I knew I couldn't take her back to her home until we were able to get rid of her carer. He had intended taking her to his doctor to have her certified the very next day, so I felt some action had to be taken. I called her solicitor who advised that we needed to have a certificate from her own doctor to show that she was still cognitively capable of making decisions. I strongly suspected that her dizziness was a result of being given the wrong dosage of her subscribed medication which he administered to her each day.

There was nowhere else for her to go, so I took her home with me. My son happened to be visiting at the time and offered to come back to Pat's home to collect some of her belongings. We found a note from the carer.

"Dear Pat, your dinner is in the microwave. Just put it on medium for five minutes. I'll be home later." The next day I was sorry that I hadn't taken the dinner out of the microwave so I could have it tested, but there was so much else going on I didn't think of it until later. We left a note telling him he had to be out of the house by the morning.

We returned in the morning and found that he had already removed quite a lot of, not only his possessions but some of Pat's as well. It looked as if he was set to come back for another load, so my son changed the locks which prevented any further removal. I looked for the previous night's meal, but there was no sign of it, not even in the rubbish bin.

I waited a few days until her dizziness had abated, and she looked in better physical shape, before taking her to her own doctor for a cognitive test. It was rather humiliating for me because she answered most questions better than I may have, so was well and truly deemed competent.

Our visit to her solicitor revealed that this man had complete control of her affairs. He was her power of attorney, power of enduring guardianship, a signatory to her advanced health directive and wait for it – he was the sole beneficiary of her will. Twenty-four hours earlier, he had planned to get a certificate to say that she was incompetent to make decisions and he would have had absolute control and life would have been hell on earth for her.

Ten harrowing days followed when, because of her intense fear, she wouldn't let me out of her sight. She would even follow me to the bathroom. It was very difficult to get things happening, so it was a relief when we were able to arrange a few weeks respite to allow me to make some arrangements for her.

Once she was settled into her temporary care facility, she gave me permission to get her house ready for sale. I had no idea what I had let myself in for as I discovered there didn't seem to be any willing helpers around, so it became my task to sort through twenty-five years of stuff and weed out enough to furnish a little one bedroom unit. She showed no interest in the process even though I offered to take her over to the house each day. It was a huge task, and I put all unwanted articles into the carport with a sign for people to take what they wanted. To my amazement, I was somehow able to source the energy I desperately required for such a mammoth task. Within a week, the house was ready for sale. Because of its location, it quickly sold and allowed me to buy the unit where I hoped Pat would find peace and safety.

Pat's grief over the sale of her beloved home and personal belongings was evident which explained why she didn't want to accompany me during the preparation for sale. I was aware of how stressful the whole process was for her and did my best to accommodate. There was also the added grief that her much-cherished dog was no longer there. Her biggest underlying grief was that the man she had trusted and grown to love had betrayed her. She found this a very hard reality to come to terms with.

It was particularly distressing to go through all her personal effects and the life she had shared with my ex-husband, John. When I found bags of new makeup in her bathroom, it triggered another wave of empathy. She had never worn makeup and I had a strong feeling that she had bought it in an attempt to make herself more attractive to the man who had been trying to strip her of everything of any value. She had allowed him free rein on her resources. Later, I had calculated that he had already helped himself to a large amount of her savings and certainly had plans to procure the rest. Because she had given him lavish gifts and free access, there was not a lot we could do to have him charged at that time, although we did report him to authorities. I suspect he has since moved on to sweet talk some other frail old lady.

I certainly hadn't nominated myself for the responsibility of looking after Pat, but she had no one else. My children were her stepchildren, and even though they were not particularly close, they agreed that it was our responsibility. Unfortunately, two of them lived overseas at that time, and the other was tied up in Brisbane. Still, we had each other's support. I thought to myself that this would make a good story, *How I Inherited My Ex-husband's Wife*. A 'who done it', or 'who almost 'done' it! It was necessary for me to put my own grief on hold and focus on assisting Pat to find a safe place.

We were relieved when she moved into her lovely little unit in a care facility. This facility had been chosen because it offered end of life care, so we felt that this meant that she could be there safely for the rest of her life. Not only was she coping with the grief of leaving her lovely home, but she continued to mourn for her little dog. As she had a tiny courtyard, she was permitted to have a small animal, so my granddaughter went into overdrive to locate a suitable dog. When seven-year-old Alfie, a beautiful little wire-haired Jack Russell, was located, Pat's future seemed to look much brighter. I should have realised that there is never a quick fix, and this certainly turned out to be the case. Little Alfie was so happy to have a new home. He would jump on Pat's knee and lick her face, but sadly she didn't really bond with him as she had with her beloved Timmy.

Pat set up her unit with furniture we had chosen from her previous home. She had a natural homemaking ability, and everyone commented on how lovely it looked. It took some time for her to feel confident enough to make her way down to the dining room for lunch using her walker, but she was not making a great deal of effort to join in the activities that were available. Her little dog served as an excuse for her not joining in. She complained a lot, telling me that everyone was suffering from dementia. By this time, I suspected that there were signs of her own failing cognitive ability, but at least she felt safe.

It was difficult to find a suitable doctor for her and the doctor she'd helped to make rich over the years with her many visits, was too far away. She didn't want a woman doctor or anyone with dark skin. After a lengthy search, I found that within the area she had moved to, there were not a lot of choices. Eventually, she settled for the resident doctor who, although being of Indian descent and dark-skinned, managed to charm her by letting her touch his luxurious mop of hair.

With her settled into a place where she had constant care, I felt able to go on a pre-planned trip overseas for a few weeks. It had been a difficult time, and I was ready for a break. I organised for my daughter to be a point of contact while I was away. Vicki visited frequently and took Pat for several outings including to a pancake parlour. Even though she had been grumpy whenever I took her for an outing, she seemed to enjoy her time with Vicki and Vicki's reports were quite positive.

Consequently, when I rang Pat on my return, I was expecting things to go on as normal.

When I called her, she was very excited to hear from me. My daughter had shown her my holiday photos which I had posted on Facebook, but when I asked her about what she had seen, she couldn't even remember my daughter visiting. A little concerned, I promised to visit her the next day.

Sadly, I was shocked at what I found. Physically she looked much better, but as soon as I arrived, Pat pulled me into the unit and whispered that we could not talk as there were conspiracy cameras in the room and she wanted to leave. She said she didn't want to be there anymore and wanted to swap her unit for one further down the coast. I promised her that we could work on finding her a place closer to where I lived.

Pat had a son who lived overseas. Over the years I knew her, she was in touch sporadically and had visited him with John, but sadly most of her relationships were tenuous as she always found much to criticise. I kept in touch with him, letting him know when there were any changes. He appeared to be grateful. However there was never any contact made by him or his family, not even a card. When I began to be concerned about her health, I suggested that she call him, but she didn't want to. There was a very sad story attached to this relationship, but I do not feel it is my place to divulge it and of course she cannot give me her permission. Suffice to say that when she told me some of the things that had happened to her, my heart went out to her and we both shed tears. Knowing a little of her background certainly helped me understand some of her behaviours.

It was after this I began to see a decline in her health. At first, I hadn't realised how much she had deteriorated cognitively, so I attempted to reason with her paranoia, with no success. She said people were breaking into her unit and stealing her band-aids and her dog's lead. This was very concerning, especially when I heard later that she had been found in the waiting room one night, covered in band-aids.

One afternoon, we attended a musical performance within the complex, and she insisted on taking the band-aids and dog's lead to stop further theft. She sang along and seemed quite happy until she stood up abruptly and said we had to leave as she had a dog to look after. I noticed that the little dog was scratching her legs and she mentioned that he needed his nails clipped and his coat trimmed, so a grooming session was arranged for little Alfie.

I managed to get an appointment with the resident doctor, he of the luxurious locks. I was hoping for a referral to a geriatrician, in order to get some advice on how she could be helped with the paranoia that was severely affecting her quality of life. It became noticeable that she had lost interest in dear little Alfie. My heart sank when she came with me to pick him up after his grooming session. Even though he emerged looking extremely handsome and with a vigorously wagging tail, she showed no interest when he proudly ran up to her.

We visited the doctor in the afternoon and after explaining my concerns asked him for a referral. Instead he and Pat began a flirtatious dialogue.

"You're alright aren't you, Patty?" She assured him she was and proceeded to joke with him.

"Everyone thinks I've gone mad, but I haven't, have I?" It was as if a different woman had changed places with her, almost as if she had become a shape-shifter. It reminded me of a few years earlier when my husband's brain tumour was causing him to exhibit some bizarre behaviour at home. Even when we visited the doctor, Mick could always be the charming gentleman, and the doctor would not believe me when I was trying to explain what was happening. So, history seemed to be repeating itself. I felt quite angry and said I would be in touch.

The very next day, Pat had a heart attack and was hospitalised. Immediately she exhibited very strange, confused behaviour and was referred to a geriatrician. He diagnosed her with a severe case of delirium and explained the differences between depression, dementia and delirium. I have since done some more research and found that sometimes they can be mistaken for each other. Apparently, delirium is not uncommon in people with some degree of dementia. I had to acknowledge there had been signs of dementia, but she had been reasonably cognitively astute until quite recently. Cognitive change in older adults can result in an added layer of acute confusion (delirium), depression, dementia and/or a combination of these.

It was heartbreaking to watch her rapid decline. One day when I visited, she had a moment of lucidity. I was surprised when she said "You are so good to me. I've never done anything for you. Why are you so good to me?" Whilst there had been moments of aggravation on my part, at that moment I looked at this small, rather shrivelled, silver-haired woman and it was as if I was seeing right into her soul. My heart overflowed, and I found myself saying it was because I loved her, and at that moment I realised that I had indeed grown to love her. She told me she loved me too. It was a special moment and probably the last rational one that I witnessed.

As well as the delirium, she was also diagnosed with vascular dementia, and then I knew that she would never go back to her lovely little unit and a new home would need to be found for darling little Alfie. I had placed him temporarily into kennels close to where I lived, but when I knew that he would never return to live with Pat, I took him home with me where he snuggled in beside me at night. He was in need of affection and re-assurance. Unfortunately, I could not keep him, but my daughter was able to find a perfect home for him with a lovely woman who could not have afforded the five hundred dollars that had been paid to the RSPCA for Alfie. We had tried him with another family, but it became obvious that he was nervous and unsettled. As soon as he spotted the lady who became his new owner, he ran to her, wagging his tail and her response to him was instant. I found it hard to say goodbye to the dear little chap, but we knew that he was going to a home where he would be loved and cared for.

Pat became a problem patient in the hospital. Her doctor would call me and say we needed to have a chat about our 'favourite patient'. I had a meeting with the care team who told me that it was my responsibility to find a suitable placement for her as she could no longer stay in the hospital. However she couldn't go anywhere until she was stabilised.

Another poignant moment happened when I took in a stuffed toy dog. It was one that she used to keep on her bed. I thought she might find comfort from having it with her. She was delighted at first, but a few days later she had buried the dog under her blanket. When she saw me, she retrieved the bedraggled toy from under the covers and begged me to take it home. She said she couldn't look after it anymore and it was fretting and wouldn't eat. There was evidence around the dog's mouth that she had been trying to feed it and was distressed that it was not complying. Once again, I experienced a wave of sadness.

Watching her deterioration was deeply affecting me. Although she was not my relative, my heart went out to those who have to see a loved one become a different person. I had recently completed a grief counselling course, and my exposure to this devastating illness heightened my desire to be able to assist others who experience many types of grief.

It became evident that she could no longer live in the little unit and I was not completely impressed with the expensive care they were offering her. After many discussions with her geriatrician, it was up to me to find a suitable place for her to go to when she was well enough to leave the hospital. Because of her difficult behaviour, no facility I approached was open to taking her. It was a very disillusioning experience. I eventually needed to hire a broker to assist me in the difficult task of finding a suitable placement. She was temporarily housed in a depressing unit beside the hospital, and every time I visited, she would yell at me that it was all my fault she was stuck there. She could not know how her behaviour was making it difficult to find her a home.

Eventually, a place was found which was, unfortunately, one hour's drive from my home. It was a new facility which I found to be horribly sterile. Pat was due to arrive at her new home the next day, so I did what I could to make it as homely as possible with colourful cushions, her soft toys and photos which did little to relieve the sterility of the room. I was not allowed to hang any pictures, so the walls remained bare and uninviting.

Upon her arrival in an ambulance, I was there to welcome her, but her delirium caused her to be more difficult than usual. I was mortified when she spat at me and told me that I was ugly. The matron assured me that she was ill and when they stabilised her and cured the delirium, she would be much better.

When I had visited this facility before Pat's move, I was told that she would be given activities to do, but every time I visited, she was strapped in a chair and pushed under a table with a colouring book and pencils to occupy herself. I told the staff that up until four weeks previously I had still been buying her crossword puzzle books. Pat had always loved doing crosswords, now she was reduced to colouring, further exacerbating her deterioration. She had quickly become institutionalised and lost the ability to walk or do any of the tasks that she was doing in her little unit. It was heartbreaking, but now with the delirium gone, she was always happy to see me.

Pat had always enjoyed a cup of coffee, but now a thickening agent of some kind was added, so it was no longer liquid. When I asked why this was the case, the staff told me that it was to help her swallow and prevent choking. She was very upset that, unlike most of the other women's meals, her food was always mushy. I was never really given a satisfactory reason for this, and I confess that whenever I took her out, I made sure she had proper coffee and food that she enjoyed and could still swallow easily. I can understand that in these types of facilities, there needs to be care taken to protect themselves from any litigation whereas I was able to take the risk in order to give her a positive experience.

It was becoming more difficult to take her on outings as she was by that time confined to a wheelchair. My back has never quite recovered from getting her and her wheelchair into my quite small car, but it was worth the effort. At this stage, although she had recovered from the delirium, her dementia had worsened, and her disposition was still far from sunny. I wanted her to have as much quality of life as possible, but she was very difficult to please.

In an effort to keep her cognition as sharp as possible, I made her a book with photos of people and places she had visited over the years. She loved it and was able to tell me who everyone was, including her son. I had managed to locate only one photo of him and was glad when she immediately knew who he was. Pat also loved looking at pictures of the places she had visited, but when she saw a photo of the lovely place she and John had lived in for many years, she became very sad. She loved the pictures of John (my ex-husband) and proudly showed the nursing staff.

When her behaviour improved, I sought approval to have her moved to a facility close to my home so it would be easier to spend more time with her. I loved the atmosphere of the place I chose. It was an older complex, but at least I was permitted to hang pictures and make it into a little home for her. I described to her the new cosy place and told her that the staff members appeared to be warm and friendly. The pièce de résistance for her was that there were men also living in the complex. Pat still liked to have men around, and there were none in her present abode.

Her furniture and paintings were in storage, so I began taking them to what I hoped would be her final resting place. My daughter and I visited her the day before her move so Vicki could cut her hair. Normally, the well-dressed women in her unit would be sitting sedately, talking to themselves or just wandering around. This day they were screaming at each other, and I witnessed some pinching and hair pulling. The staff just rolled their eyes and blamed it on the full moon. Pat, sitting in her chair, wisely informed us, "We're all mad in here you know." She said it with such wry humour we couldn't help laughing with her.

Once more I felt immense compassion and totally forgave her for the difficult behaviour she so often exhibited. How could I know what this frail, little woman had experienced? I assured her that things were looking up as we were going to move her to a happier place.

The next morning, I went to pick up the remainder of her belongings from storage, thinking to put the finishing touches to her room. A phone call abruptly ended my vision of making a better life for her. The call was from a doctor in the intensive care unit at the hospital where Pat had previously been treated. The doctor advised me that Pat was in a coma and I should come straight away. With a heavy heart, I abandoned my plans and drove directly to the hospital.

In the intensive care unit, I found Pat struggling for breath and was told that she had little time left. I resolved to stay with her as I have always felt that no one deserves to die alone. She was moved up into a room for end-of-life care. The staff made me up a very uncomfortable day bed making it possible for me to stay with her all that night and the next day until a member of staff complained, and the bed was removed.

There was no change in her condition all the next day. I needed to sleep but was concerned that she would die alone. The man in the next room had passed away the night before, and I was touched by the fact that he was surrounded by many family members, so I was not prepared to leave her.

The next day she opened her eyes and seemed very alert. I had rung her son, and suddenly there was some communication from him and his family. I told her that they had sent her love, she smiled and I could see that she understood. Something told me to assure her that it was okay to let go, her time of suffering was over. She nodded and spent the next few days at peace but with eyes wide open, very much alert. It was lovely to see this woman, who had been so difficult and irritable most of the time I had known her, transformed into a vision of peace. All the lines on her face appeared to be ironed out and the often grumpy face had been replaced by softness and a slight smile. On my phone, I still keep a photo of her taken at that time.

My daughter came to the hospital to relieve me so that I could rest. A little time later she rang to tell me that it was a special experience to spend time with someone so close to death. There was a tranquil feeling in the air, and she was able to tell Pat that her angel had come for her. Pat smiled and fell asleep.

That night, I slept nearby at my grandson's home. It was hard to say how long Pat would remain in this condition, but the next morning when I returned to the hospital, I immediately knew there was a change. Previously her head had been turned towards the window, and she seemed to be seeking something there, but as I walked in, the first thing I noticed was that her head was facing the door making her face visible as soon as I walked in. I was a little shocked to see that her face had transformed from the serenity of the day before. It was obvious that her life had almost slipped away. As I came closer and hugged her, I could see her face visibly relax. I wonder if she was concerned that I wouldn't be there. She was still breathing, but I knew her time was near.

Nobody can prepare themselves for this moment. I thought I had been ready for Mick's passing but was not ready for the rush of emotion I had felt, and now I was facing another person's death, this time with very mixed emotions. It had been a tough year, and now it was coming to an end. This woman whom I had found difficult to like at times, had consumed so much of my thoughts and time, yet through it all, I had grown to love her. I kissed her again, and her eyes fluttered open, I may have imagined it, but I am sure I saw a hint of a smile.

"You can let go now, Pat. Your hard days are over, and Timmy will be there to greet you," I whispered as I held her close. Half an hour later she slipped peacefully away. I felt that it was a real privilege to have shared this time with her and was surprised by the grief I felt and how freely my tears flowed.

My car was still full of her belongings. There were many loose ends to tie up. I had been robbed of this next part of the process when Mick died, but now it was my sole responsibility to organise the cremation and the completion of her death certificate. Pat's ashes were safely stored in a ceramic jar accompanied by a white rose. After speaking with my children, we decided to have a special ceremony, when the time was right, and release Pat's ashes along with some of John's. My daughter had kept some of her father's ashes for such a purpose. I always honoured that there had been love between Pat and John and it seemed only right that we remember that love at this closure of their earthly existence.

I sometimes feel that we are given the lessons we need. I learnt so much from this whole experience and saw it as part of my fabulous journey. The biggest lesson for me has been to discover that you don't have to like someone to love them and that only love is real. It also helped me to understand that it is possible to find something extraordinary in someone we may have previously dismissed.

I feel so grateful to have been able to spend those last days with her. I saw beauty where I had previously only seen anxiety and tension. I can't help feeling that in those last four days, she really found her 'fabulous'. I'm so glad that I was there to witness it. As I reflected on the year that had passed, I realised that I had put my own grief on hold.

3. LYN'S HEALING TOOLBOX

I learnt so much from this experience which I would like to share.

- Everyone has a story, and we often have no idea what they may have suffered. When someone exhibits behaviour we might find difficult, we can choose to remember that there may be a reason.
- It is possible not to like the way someone behaves, but it is still possible to love them. Pat was difficult but so very vulnerable, and I didn't find out until near the end of her life the reason for her being so difficult.
- When older people are lonely, they can become very vulnerable to others taking advantage of them. Elder abuse is sadly a very common occurrence.
- I was uncertain whether to step in when the gardener took over Pat's life, but given the same scenario, I would have no hesitation to investigate the matter and have him on police watch.
- I learnt a great deal about dementia and how it is not always possible to reason with the patient. I hadn't realised the early signs and continued to try and reason with Pat, to no avail. Remember the real person is still there.
- There is so much grief involved when a loved one has been diagnosed with dementia. I only had a small taste, but it made me want to be available to those who are seeing their loved ones diminishing before their eyes.

There are so many elements to Pat's story, such as:

- Birthing a child in her early teens;
- A mother who disowned her;
- Later moving to another country and marrying an abusive man;
- Fleeing to Australia and starting a new life;
- At last finding love and marrying a kind man who was good to her before he died;
- Meeting John and enjoying 25 years together;

- ○ Grief at the death of another loved husband;
- ○ Huge emotional abuse from a man trying to rob her of everything and we suspect, killing her beloved dog, both of which caused her so much grief.

Her own demise, heartbreak, leading to dementia and having to leave the home that she loved. There is more that I am unable to write about. I am so glad I was given the opportunity to learn to love her.

CHAPTER 4

Grief and Victimhood – a daunting combination

As a consultant working in the education system with students who did not fit that system, I met many examples of life-changing breakthroughs that taught me valuable lessons. I certainly value the resilience I witnessed as a remarkable trait. Working with students and adults as they navigate their way from tribulation to triumph has helped me to keep going when often I felt overwhelmed by the enormity of my job. As a specialist teacher, dealing with a large number of students who were struggling to find their place in the world, I needed to explore different ways of learning. There are so many stories that would fill several books, but I would just like to mention a few of the more positive ones where students went on to really find their 'fabulous' after dealing with grief.

My focus in this book is about grief in its many guises and make no mistake, I observed each of these students suffering deep grief for different reasons. The common element I found was that each of them had suffered bullying of some kind and also the indignity of being misunderstood.

There were some unusual situations to deal with as a consultant. Often I was expected to be able to wave a magic wand and make everything alright. There were magical things that did happen. It was always a joy to see how encouragement transformed some students who didn't fit into the system for some reason or another.

Sometimes the process that worked was quite simple, but at other times we had to dig deeper to find some underlying causes that might be impinging on progress. One young lad, whom I will call 'Terry', was very frustrated because he felt he couldn't learn to read. He had been born without ears and I had to hold back tears when he said that if he could learn to read, he might get new ears for Christmas. He was being bullied and whilst this was causing him a great deal of grief, it was not the reason he was having difficulty in learning to read. After some in-depth investigation, we found that he needed help from a behavioural optometrist as he was unable to track along a line. When I would slowly take my finger to his nose, his eyes would slide to the right, making it impossible to read along a line. He began working on exercises prescribed by the behavioural optometrist and the magic happened. The day he came in to see me with a big smile on his face I knew there had been a breakthrough. Clutching a book in his hand, he triumphantly announced that this was the first book he had ever been able to *really* read. Plastic surgery gave him new ears but being able to read provided him with the confidence he needed to become a successful student.

Mick always loved to hear the stories I would tell him about my students. He understood the passion I have always had to help people out of grief and victimhood. I guess it stemmed from the abuse I had suffered as a child. I wasn't always productive in the way I handled my life and have not always felt proud of some of my actions. In later years I came to understand the strength and insight I gained from every experience and how each has helped me to assist others who may be experiencing grief and victimhood.

As a consultant for exceptional children or students who didn't fit into the system, I was deeply moved when I witnessed the grief that young people suffered when they felt like outcasts because they didn't fit into an acceptable box. They often suffered intense bullying and verbal abuse.

I was privileged to have the opportunity to work with students in remote areas. I would love to tell some of these stories in more depth, but because I no longer have access to their contact information, I cannot get their permission to tell their story. What I can do is talk about my own experience in working with them and seeing them rise above their grief to step into a new way of being, which is what we all try to do while we are finding our 'fabulous'. To protect their privacy, I have changed their names.

Jim

Whilst working with remote area students, I was called upon to visit a boy who was in the middle of completing his year seven. He was struggling and totally disengaged. When I read his file and gained some insight about his situation, I could understand that there was a gap in what the education system was trying to get him to understand and what context was available to him. When you are in a classroom, you can read the students and find a way to engage them, but when they are working remotely, there has to be a different way of engaging them.

Visiting this boy, whom I will call Jim, helped me to understand the difficulties he was having. It became clear that he had spent most of his school years feeling not good enough. It was a worthwhile visit as it didn't take long to find out that there were many skills which we could work with.

The five-hour drive was shared with a companion. We wondered what we were going to find. I knew a few facts about this young man which included how good he was at fixing machinery.

We had to drive through five creek beds on the way to the farmhouse – an experience in itself. When we arrived, Jim was nowhere to be found. Eventually, I came face to face with a surly looking young man with a hard, pinched face. My heart immediately went out to him. Even though at that stage, I didn't know the extent of his story, I could read a face etched in pain.

In an attempt to start a conversation, I mentioned that I knew people who were keen to know more about fattening calves. His eyes lit up. This statement was a successful icebreaker, so when I asked him if I could see his calves, he didn't hesitate. This involved traipsing through muddy sludge and layers of excretions, but nothing was going to daunt me now. Once we had reached the calves, I watched his hard face soften as he leaned down to speak to each calf. His show of tenderness touched me, and I made a silly statement.

"It must be hard to give them up when they get too big to be here." He straightened up and his softened features immediately hardened. I regretted making that comment.

We moved around the property and I was able to observe what his real passions were, and they certainly did not include the history of the Roman Empire. However, in our conversations, I had gathered a great deal of information from him, and as we moved with his mother to the school room, I made the pronouncement that I didn't want him to do the papers anymore. With great dramatic effect, I tore up the paper that was on the desk. His face was a mixture of horror and relief. What was this mad woman doing?

I could see that the reading material provided for him was inappropriate, and I told him from now on I would source reading books that were about machinery. His English syllabus would include a weekly summary about what he had been doing on the farm each week, and from what he had written I would pick up the spelling and grammar he needed to meet the requirements for his year.

As the year went on, he made significant progress. His mother was thrilled as she had her heart set on him going to agricultural college the following year. Jim was very resistant. He had never been away from home and understandably his lack of confidence and the fear of the unknown terrified him.

I was able to have a constructive conversation with the principal of the agricultural college and we came up with the idea that if Jim could be accelerated into year nine, he would escape the number of subjects that most students in year eight have to complete in order to work out what they wanted to specialise in. Our young man already had strong ideas about what he wanted his future to look like, so it was agreed that we could trial the idea that he skip year eight. This already appealed to him and the icing on the cake was that he was given permission to take his horse with him.

I am still moved when I think of the years that followed. Not only did Jim feel very clever for having skipped a grade, the compassionate principal placed him in a strand where he succeeded in gaining As and Bs for his work. Needless to say, his mother was over the moon.

I lost sight of Jim for a few years as I moved further south to work with a different set of carnival students who moved around Australia. One day the phone rang at my desk.

"Oh Lyn, at last, I have found you." Jim's mother had been searching for me as she had some special news to tell me. "Jim has just received the award for apprentice of the year." We both cried.

For many of the students I worked with, their biggest grief was the feeling that they were not accepted by others. Every student I worked with was experiencing something different, but as I have already mentioned, the common elements were bullying, lack of understanding and low self-esteem. How can anyone find their 'fabulous' when they feel so bad about themselves? I had many discussions with teachers and the powers that be in the education world. I am excited about the fact that philosophy is being taught in a number of schools which encourages children from a young age to think for themselves. This can be very empowering. I am passionate about the importance of each person being valued for who they are and given permission to be different.

Joel

One of my very favourite young men who becomes more 'fabulous' every day, is my grandson Joel who, a bit like his grandmother, has been a late bloomer and I have no doubt will achieve great things.

He loved books from an early age and expected to go to school and simply learn to read. Alarm bells rang for me when he didn't seem to pick it up very easily, but his father was concerned that I may label him and didn't allow me to work with him. He didn't understand that many dyslexic people are highly intelligent but sadly, if not given early intervention, can go on to lose their confidence and sense of self. I believe that his difficulty in learning to read caused Joel to suffer huge grief which he was at pains to hide and he became quite angry. I have witnessed this phenomenon again and again in schools. Often the child who is acting up, being the class clown, disrupting classes or being very angry, is often a child who is covering up their angst about not understanding what is going on for them. Why can't they achieve like others in the class? Joel did have a period of being the class clown in his high school years, but in his early primary school, he acted out his frustration by being angry. He was always a loving and relatively easy child at home but at school he became an angry warrior. Mothers would complain that he had shown anger with their child and he was forbidden to play with them. This was a lonely period for him and he spent time by himself in the library.

I was concerned when in his early years at school he was so proud that some of my books were in his school library. Considering my published works were all about spelling, reading and literacy, I am ashamed to say that when he told me how proud he was, I said, "Oh you don't tell anyone I'm your grandmother do you?" The reply, "Oh yes, I tell everyone." This from a grandson who could not read and could not spell. Bang, I thought my credibility was shot. However, after many years of struggle, he has risen victorious. Things began to change for him when he was in Year 10, and I was given permission to have him assessed by a professional. His results revealed an incredibly high I.Q. but a very low reading level for his age. At the time, this was the only measure used to diagnose dyslexia. I will never forget his first words as we entered the lift, "I'm not dumb after all." My reply, "Darling nobody ever thought you were dumb." The fact that he had this belief was enough to affect him in so many areas of his life. He went on to complete his high school years and continued to study for a Diploma of Business through TAFE (Technical And Further Education).

There are many lecturers who still do not understand that students who are dyslexic, are capable of outstanding work. I have seen comments on brilliant papers such as, "It is hard to believe that English is your native language." These days, spell check has helped, but Joel found it difficult and dropped out of the course. I was extremely proud of him when he decided to go back and give it another go. Not only did he succeed in gaining his Diploma of Business, he also went on to enrol at the university for an Economics Degree. Joel began to understand how his dyslexia affected the way he read and wrote. He learnt to decode his own work and correct it, which I think is absolutely brilliant. I am so proud of him.

How can anyone find their 'fabulous' if they are not given the opportunity to recognise the skills they have. We still live in a society that focuses on our negatives rather than our positives. I have a friend who has worked in the prison system and she shared with me that there are many men and women who end up in the prison system as a result of low self-esteem and poor literacy skills.

Jeffrey

I have fond memories of Jeffrey, a snowy-haired student who was in Year 4 when he came into my realm. Jeffrey was really frustrated by his inability to read, yet he could follow diagrams and was particularly interested in electronics. His self-esteem was severely impaired by his feeling that he was 'dumb' in exactly the same way as had my grandson. Yet he could go to the dump, pick out any electronic equipment, and following diagrams he would construct the most amazing creations with impressive bells and whistles. However, the fact that he couldn't read placed him in a category that he didn't fit. It distressed me to walk past his classroom and see the invisible dunce's cap on his head as he struggled to cope with the demands of a teacher who could not comprehend that someone who couldn't read could still be highly intelligent.

When Jeffrey reached Year 7, he was placed in a class with a traditional teacher who was only interested in students who could achieve. A program called, *Tournament of the Minds* had been created by a group of lateral thinking people who recognised that some kids did not fit the educational system but could be encouraged to think outside the square. The Tournament is designed to encourage lateral thinking, creativity and teamwork skills in young people around Australia and the Pacific region. I was thrilled as it provided students with a different approach to learning and gave them useful skills in communication. This was a perfect program for students like Jeffrey. This particular year they announced a robotics competition, and I became really excited. I approached Jeffrey's teacher to suggest entering him in the competition. The teacher was rather surprised that I would consider enrolling Jeffrey in a competition he had considered was only for gifted students and he certainly did not see Jeffrey included in this category.

However, Jeffrey did enter the competition and easily won the state title. A short time later I received a call in the middle of the night. Jeffrey was calling from Melbourne where it had been announced that he had won the national title. I burst into tears as I knew this would be a new day for Jeffrey who had spent his life feeling that he was a hopeless case. There is more to his story as we followed him through his high school years where the compassionate principle agreed to read him his exam questions and record his answers.

Following were some negotiations with TAFE (Technical And Further Education) who initially said they could not enrol a student who was unable to read into an electrical engineering course. Many years later, we can report that he did indeed find his 'fabulous'. This 'dumb' kid now owns his own electrical engineering shop as well as being a champion triathlete. I shudder when I think of how his life could have been, yet it saddens me to think of how many are robbed of their 'fabulous' because of lack of understanding and knowledge of who they really are.

Martha

Martha came to my attention when a teacher asked me to be involved. She felt that Martha was perhaps a little backward, possibly even 'mentally retarded', and she wasn't sure how she could be helped. My companion and I drove many hours to the property which was quite isolated. On our arrival, we found a very nervous little girl and an equally nervous mother.

After some discussion, my companion and I both realised that instead of being backward, we were dealing with a child who was quite brilliant. What had happened was again caused by the inability to easily have a face to face discussion with students. These days this is achieved via the internet which was not available to these students at that time.

There was a marking system which was rigidly adhered to by some teachers, and because Martha initially answered questions that were outside the prescribed answer, her answers would be marked wrong. This resulted in Martha feeling that she was unable to answer questions correctly and so stopped answering them at all. This was another occasion when I took it upon myself to take her off the traditional papers and give her open-ended questions so that she could really use her out-of-the box thinking. I asked her to write a book about what would happen to the world if it was taken over by robots. One of the other activities was to design a piece of equipment that would help her mother on the farm.

Martha diligently set to work and wrote and illustrated a book that was of a very high standard. It was innovative and exciting. I read it to the staff of this school and told them that the author was only eight. There were cries of amazement. "What a gifted child." My reply was, "Oh no, this child has been deemed to be backward." It was a great opportunity to explain that we sometimes need to look deeper to see what might be hindering a child's progression.

When I left education, I worked in big corporations and I believe the same rule applies. I saw people who thought differently being pushed aside when I know that, given the opportunity, they had much to offer.

Martha also excelled in her design of a chook feeder for her mother. I think the design should have been patented, but I couldn't get any traction on that idea. However, she went on to excel, particularly when she went to boarding school and became dux of the school. I'd love to know where she is now, but I am pretty confident that with her mother's support and a new understanding about herself, she will have found her niche.

Indigenous Students

The world would be such a wonderful place if people would let go of judgement and practice acceptance and love. I am happy that it is now accepted in most schools that there are different types of learners. This knowledge led to me writing the series, "Thinking Sideways" in order to encourage children to think more broadly. (See reference section)

I loved working with Indigenous students. They thrived on open-ended activities. The opportunity to use some of Edward De Bono's strategies with Indigenous students always yielded some exciting and unexpected results. (For more information see reference section at the end of this book) I remember taking a group of children for a session where we used the PMI (Plus, Minus or Interesting). We started with some basic situations like a walk in the bush where they discussed the plus, minus and interesting things that came out of this activity. We then moved onto subjects that they chose. We often collapsed into laughter at some of the answers. I really enjoyed these sessions.

The guidance officer, the community leader and I, working collaboratively, managed to achieve a breakthrough when we changed the method of learning for our Indigenous students. I found it exciting to explore new ways which involved getting their parents and young people into the schools and working with them together to construct programs which would suit the learning styles of their children. As a result, I was given permission to train unemployed Indigenous youth to work one-on-one with young students. They had a full week of intensive training after which they graduated with a certificate and a badge that said, "Teacher's Aid". For some this was the only recognition they had received in their whole life and they proudly clutched their certificates. It was great to see some improvement in their behaviour. Self-esteem issues were dealt with as these new 'Teacher's Aids' helped their students to succeed. The program worked well because it was designed together with parents and students. Working one on one with young people who understood their culture made a world of difference.

Some of the older Aboriginal students were causing havoc in the classroom. My experience, as I have previously mentioned, has found that this behaviour usually stems from lack of self-esteem. When they were given tasks that made them feel important, their behaviour changed. Peer tutoring was a big success. I was able to train older students who struggled with their literacy, to become 'tutors' for younger students. Every Wednesday, they would go to the younger student's classrooms to collect their 'tutees'. They organised a folder for each student in which they charted their progress as they worked through a box of books chosen by the student. Together we had made books constructed by the older students and collected from their oral stories and chants. I made them into big books which they illustrated. There was so much enthusiasm and class behaviour improved along with their literacy skills. We had students lining up to be on the program. This was a unique and special time of my life and my heart swells every time I think about it. There is still so much that needs to be done but I am optimistic about the future.

This chapter has been referring to a completely different form of grief. I have witnessed many young people experiencing so much unnecessary grief. I am sure that if I had not had similar experiences as a child, I couldn't have understood the depth of their grief. Something I did have to learn was to become a little more detached. At first, I found my compassion went into overdrive, and when that happens, we can become ineffective. I am not sure why there are some people who find it difficult to provide encouragement and validation.

In some ways, it is similar to my experience with Pat. It is so easy to have a perception about somebody that can be totally inaccurate. Grief can cause people to behave in all sorts of protective behaviour. Our most important task is to listen.

> I need you to listen to me
> No one has listened to me
> No one understands my suffering
> Including the ones who say they love me.
> The pain inside me is suffocating me.
> It is the TNT that makes up the bomb.
> By Thich Nhat Hanh – *Call Me by My True Names.*

For listening is the act of entering the skin of the other and wearing it for a time as if it were our own. Listening is the gateway to understanding.
David Spangler, *Parent as Mystic, Mystic as Parent*

4. LYN'S HEALING TOOLBOX

Our children and young people are our hope for the future, and there is much we can do to help them find their own *fabulous*. It is important that we seek to understand.

- Listening is an important component for assisting anyone with their grief. The importance of listening is often underestimated when it comes to children and young people. There will be times that they do not want to talk and other forms of observation need to come into play.

- It is so easy to criticise but remember that one word of encouragement is more valuable than a barrowful of negatives. This doesn't mean that we lay on the positives when we know that they are not making an effort.

- If children are taught to be able to identify their feelings when young, it helps them to be more in tune as adults. I am loving that many schools now are introducing philosophy and self-awareness. As an outsider, I was able to get these students to tell me how they felt, and it often broke my heart, but that is when it is important to show empathy rather than sympathy, and sometimes this requires a bit of tough love.

- I have mainly mentioned learning difficulties, but any child/adult who is different will crave to be treated like everybody else. Once the difference is identified, it is better if there is transparency as we work together for a solution. These case studies were all gifted in their own way.
    - Most felt they were misunderstood and not being heard;
    - Joel was devastated when his longing to be able to read was not realised, and he acted out in anger so that people wouldn't notice;
    - Jeffrey had an incredibly scientific mind, but his extreme dyslexia caused him to be labelled 'dumb'.
    - Martha excelled when she was given permission to expand her thinking.
    - As educators, we need to be open to the fact that some children require the opportunity to explore a different

method of learning. This was certainly the case with my Indigenous students. They flourished when given an opportunity to learn in their own way.

- With encouragement, and when the time was right, each of them was able to tell me how they were feeling. This was a new experience as sometimes they would just act out without knowing why.
- It is important that we recognise our role is to support and assist but not to 'fix'. I have found that each child, whatever their experience, is our teacher and it is beneficial if we are adults that are willing to be taught.

CHAPTER 5

Finding My Feet

L ooking back, I can acknowledge that whilst there were a few times I felt I hadn't succeeded, I did manage to turn around quite a few negative circumstances. It now seems strange to me as I could always fight assertively for the rights of any student or adult in the workplace, but I did not acknowledge that Lyn Traill also had rights and abilities. I did not love or nurture her as she deserved to be nurtured and it has taken many years of persistence to learn the importance and the skills which have allowed me to move towards what I could accept as my true fabulous.

At this time, I was simply devoted to gaining positive outcomes for marginalised students and adults. Unconsciously I was reliving my own childhood pain of never feeling good enough and desperately wanting to alleviate the pain for others. I would fight for their rights, but when I became the butt of others criticism of my methods, I would doubt my own intuition. I guess I so desperately wanted the approval of everybody. When I read the following quote by Jeanette Winterson, it rang so true for me.

> "I've always tried to make a home for myself, but I have
> not felt at home in myself. I've worked hard at being the
> hero of my own life. But every time I checked the register

of displaced persons, I was still on it. I didn't know how to belong. Longing? Yes. Belonging? No."
—Jeanette Winterson, Why Be Happy When You Could Be Normal?

I felt that I was a long way from finding my fabulous.

I've spent a long time reflecting on the years I had spent working with so many students and adults and wondering how they had all fared in the ensuing years. I made the mistake of remembering the many critics who had been so willing to put me down. Of course, I didn't realise at that time I had made myself the willing target. I was given some amazing opportunities and yet, like Jeanette, I still felt like a displaced person.

Mick came galloping into my life like a knight in shining armour. He was so grounded and oozing in confidence that at first, he couldn't believe that I was not the same. He had been impressed that I had a number of published works and had managed to run my own business, yet I almost saw my successes as flukes. I would think to myself that one day, he would realise that I am not the amazingly successful person that he thinks I am. The imposter syndrome was at that time well and truly alive.

It was not long after we met that I was given the opportunity to study for a Graduate Diploma in Ontological Coaching. At the time, I had been running my own training and coaching company for the previous nine years. Two of those years had been spent working as a manager at a business training college which had been a steep learning curve. A big turning point for me was the self-knowledge engendered by this powerful study of an in-depth coaching practice. I learnt more about myself in those eighteen months of study than I had in all of my previous years. I hadn't realised how I was still locked into the moods of resentment about my troubled childhood; resignation that I was not good enough, and anxiety about the future. I embraced the program with tremendous zeal and found myself becoming a better observer of my behaviour and the person I had become. Mick noticed a significant change and encouraged me to write a book about it. It was with his encouragement that *Sizzling at Seventy – Victim to Victorious* was born. It was thrilling to have it published before his death. He was so proud when the first box of books arrived.

I guess I thought I was further ahead than I really was because following Mick's death I fell in a heap. This brought on deep feelings of guilt. I felt like I had let down the clients I had helped with my coaching. I must say that things would have been much worse for me without the strategies I had previously gained, but I now realise that I still had many steps to take before I would believe that I had found my fabulous.

Whilst I had learnt so much from taking care of Pat, I was now left with a bit of an empty hole. Once more I had to confront the waves of sadness that invaded my soul. They would come upon me at unbidden moments, and the tears would flow. I threw myself into my work and a few years after Mick's death I met a lovely man called John. The sadness didn't go away, but as I have said before, the spaces in between stretched further apart.

John was tall, intelligent and attractive. He taught me the valuable lesson that you never love someone the same way twice, and it is possible to love again. He was supportive, and I will always be grateful for the special times we had together, but I now believe we were both in post grief states. Whilst he gave me a wonderful outlet for my grief, I think in many ways he was suffering more than he was able to admit. We had a special trip to Europe together which will always remain one of the highlights of my life, but we returned home to lots of unresolved stuff and different expectations of the relationship.

In the confusion of it all, I made another escape, and this one was more difficult than I could have imagined. It was an escape into physical pain. There was still something more to learn before I would be completely set free.

5. LYN'S HEALING TOOLBOX

Some of us were brought up in an era when it was drilled into us to not love ourselves. We must instead be humble and ask for forgiveness for any perceived wrong thought or act. This has caused a great deal of confusion, and it is exciting to know that it is never too late to reverse these teachings.

- It is important to acknowledge the strengths we have. Sometimes it is helpful for someone who knows you well to help you list them. I was in a vulnerable place when someone helped me to do this, and I felt a bit embarrassed at first. It is much easier to point out faults than strengths.
- Go back to the mood framework and observe if there is a mood that is not serving you. If there is, work on how you can reverse the mood to a more positive one. It's important to observe breathing and posture. Becoming better observers of ourselves, and what we stand for, is very freeing.
- I remember being told to look in the mirror and to tell myself repeatedly that I love myself. I found this difficult at first as I resisted the notion that it is okay for me to love myself, when in fact, it is more than okay. It is crucial if we are going to believe that we have found our fabulous.
- It has taken me so long to understand that when people criticise your work or actions, it is often their stuff. The tall poppy syndrome is sadly alive and well. Once we learn to follow our own intuition, remember that our thoughts and language create our reality, and accept the law of attraction, we can dismiss criticism from others. Of course, we can always welcome other points of view and discern what will work for us.
- Be honest with yourself about why you are taking on other people's stuff or acting in ways that are stunting your growth and not helping you to progress. Sometimes another person or persons can help, but it has been exciting for me to find that once we are really in touch with ourselves – even in our grief – there will come a time when we will be confident enough to fly

on our own. If others are part of that, they become the icing on the cake.

- Part of being fabulous is being able to be genuinely happy for the success of others.

CHAPTER 6

Stripped Bare

While working through my grief, I will always treasure the few years I spent as a contract coach in a large organisation where I was shown a great deal of respect. I now believe that I became far too entrenched in the office politics and I should have heeded some warnings that I felt intuitively. I have had to be hit over the head with a metaphorical hammer to remind myself how important it is for me to believe my gut feelings. However, I needed to go through some challenging experiences until I finally got the message, *"Lyn, listen to your gut for goodness sake!"* I stuck my nose into something that was concerning me for the organisation and, even though my intentions were honourable, they backfired in a big way. During a business trip to Fiji on an assignment, the work colleague I was concerned about took the opportunity to turn everything around and make it my fault. The sense of betrayal was huge, but then, I had only myself to blame, and I chose to say goodbye to the organisation.

The sense of loss was enormous, and I now believe that the accumulation of past betrayals had banked up and I needed to deal with the part I had played in them, albeit unwittingly. I was totally devastated, and there was a big dent in my pride. I honestly didn't know what to do next so, unconsciously, I escaped into pain.

I have always been rather smug about my ability to ride through pain. As a rough and tumble female, I have sustained many injuries over the years. My response to a dare to jump over a cliff as a child had caused ongoing back problems which I had learned to manage even when x-rays revealed that I should be less mobile than I am. I have never let pain stop me from doing anything I wanted to do until I was faced with chronic, debilitating pain. What had happened to invincible Lyn? I was in agony and didn't want people to know what I was experiencing. I would pack pillows all around me because even the slightest movement would send arrows of pain darting around my body. This was completely different from the pain I suffered immediately following losing Mick.

I've never felt afraid of death, and one night I thought maybe it was time I let go – fade into the never, never, and float into the night. The persistent pain of the previous year had worn me down, and it seemed as if there was no remedy. I certainly gained a better understanding and empathy for chronic pain sufferers becoming addicted to their pain relief, but I didn't want to go down that path.

As I lay there with pillows packed around me, I made a declaration.

"I think I will die tonight!" It felt like it might be the right time. I had done my hard yards, and I was ready. Sad music, please. I had tried so hard to write my follow-up book, but everything I wrote sounded so trite and formulaic. I'd attempted to write Donna Cooper's amazing story and the work she is doing in Cambodia. I had committed myself to this task and even envisioned it as a movie with Angelina Jolie playing Donna. I hope one day this will happen, maybe not with Angelina, but it is a remarkable story. However, as things unfolded, it became obvious that this was not going to be my role. Circumstances decreed otherwise, and with a heavy heart, I reluctantly scrapped the project. However, Donna has given me permission to share some of her story which I have done later in the book.

I tried going back to where I had left off with my previous book, *Sizzling at Seventy*, but it just wasn't happening so I felt it was all over for me. I had gained no clients in the previous year, and the little pieces of work I had done did not lead to anything significant. I did manage to ghostwrite a book on Social Media which caused much hilarity amongst the trenches as previously Lyn and Social Media were complete aliens. However, whilst it did not give me much personal satisfaction, it did pay for a new lounge suite, which we enjoy. It seemed to me that my life, as

I had known it, was over and it was time to give myself permission to leave this mortal coil.

I felt quite peaceful laying there waiting for everything to shut down. I could feel myself floating into a state that felt as if I was between two worlds. It was reminiscent of the feeling I had so many years ago when I was given a choice between living and dying. Strangely it was a good feeling. Suddenly human thinking intervened in the process. It seems funny now, but I remembered that I had left my bathroom in a mess and other unfinished business came to mind. Would I like to leave this earth in such an unfinished state? Rational thought won out, and I decided that leaving an untidy bathroom was not ideal, so perhaps I would not die tonight after all. I still believe I was given a choice that night.

Now was the time I needed to concentrate on another choice. If I was going to live, what was I going to do? I didn't intend to live as I had for the previous year, in a great deal of pain and achieving very little. I was aware of the psychological effects of chronic pain, and there were times when I thought I had lost the plot. I had read that *"Pain catastrophising involves the magnification of pain symptoms leading to increased levels of depression, an increased sense of helplessness, anxiety and consequent functional loss.* (Block and Cianfrini) Could it be possible that I had become someone who was actually pain catastrophising? Perish the thought! In the past I have coached people with chronic pain, thinking that I understood what they were going through and could help them. But, apparently, I needed to go through a much deeper experience, and now I understand so much more about what it feels like to suffer chronic pain.

My son Matt reminded me to change my language. Whilst I was recovering from whatever was happening to my body, Matt often reminded me that I used the words, "I can't". I thought he was a bit harsh, but I began consciously to change my language to "Yes I CAN!" Guess what? It worked. I began to see that most of my "I can't" dialogue became "Yes I can", and I found myself doing things I thought I could no longer do. Why should I be surprised when I had trained others in the concept of *'Language Creates Our Reality'*. It also seemed to be the proof I needed that our bodies can regenerate, and we can do far more than we think we ever could. It was also time to revisit any material I had on '*The Law of Attraction*'. I can't believe that I had lost sight of this glorious concept and began to embrace it in a totally new way.

As new perspectives and opportunities now come into my realm, I am grateful to Matt for being so firm with me. He has overcome so much himself, so I should not have hesitated to give him the authority to be firm with me. I really needed that wake-up call.

It was time to take stock and get moving again. In my meditations I poured out my heart, begging to be surrounded by people who could help me transition into a more positive role. I don't understand why it took me so long to get to that point unless it was necessary for me to understand how easily we can sabotage ourselves. Already I have found this experience beneficial in my coaching practice. Going through an experience certainly makes a difference when coaching others not to fall into the same traps. Although I am thankful for my deeper understanding after having gone through such an experience, I secretly hope there is a limit to further experiences.

It wasn't long before my plea for guidance was answered, and unexpectedly new people came into my life. Each individual has had something different to teach me. It took me a while to grasp that was the case. It was almost as if I had to go back to baseline. I was stripped bare. I found myself swallowing my pride and embracing some new approaches, some of which I ultimately found necessary to discard. I beat myself up a lot and tended to discount any successes of the past. It was a strange but wonderful place to be in, and I am thankful to those who hung in there with the belief that I had much to offer.

It seemed that there were so many people offering me solutions and I began to feel overwhelmed as I sorted out the steps I should take. Mardy Penrose has given me permission to write about my experience with her. She took me back to basics. However, when she mentioned the word goals, I froze, thinking of the years when that was the buzzword and remembering when that very word made me cringe. However, Mardy's skilful approach in assisting me to look at my future with fresh eyes unlocked all of my resistance. I began to value myself as a successful woman who had accomplished so much. I was able to recognise that there was still much for me to do and Mardy was persistent in making me work hard to not only set intentions but to specify the steps I needed to take.

It was wonderful to have someone believe in me so much, but I needed to take that belief out of the cognitive domain and into my heart. I had closed my heart off so many times. I was finding it difficult to open it enough to allow myself to totally embrace the notion that I was the remarkable woman Mardy believed me to be. There was still so much resistance, and I didn't understand where it was coming from.

It was time for another lesson, and by default, I attended a day seminar with my daughter. I was relishing spending the day with her rather than whatever content was going to be made available. Michelle Cannan presented, 'The Soul Apprenticeship – Mastering the Human Experience' which is a proven five-step process that teaches you how unwanted life cycles are the pathway to unlocking frustrating, recurring blocks in your personal, professional and financial experiences. No one was more surprised than me when I was given a message that I should enrol in her five-week course. At first, the cynic in me made a weak attempt to fight it.

In the first session we were asked to declare what it was that we were ready to transform, and immediately I identified that I wanted to completely eradicate any self-doubt that seemed to still haunt me, and I wanted to be able to undertake any task that was part of my purpose. Now that I was feeling better, what I needed more than anything else was to spend the rest of my days doing meaningful work. I didn't realise that I had partly slipped back into the old mood of resignation that I had worked hard to eradicate before my husband's death. I wanted to get my book written and continue to coach and go on speaking tours. However, I kept questioning whether I was too old or good enough? These doubts were weighing me down, and I was keen to take them off the radar.

Michelle was inspired to create a five-step process, and I came to understand why it was called The Soul Apprenticeship. One activity had us identify our treasure word which is our soul value. Everyone else in the group seemed to identify a word quite quickly whilst my word evaded me. I was still relying too much on the cognitive process which really suited my work with Mardy, but now I was being asked to open my heart and embrace my true identity. It seemed like I needed a big old wrench to pry open this heart of mine. It would make tentative little efforts to open right up and then snap shut again.

One morning I woke up and the word that came to me was, 'authenticity', and as I spoke the word aloud, I felt my heart open up in a way I hadn't experienced for quite a long time. Why had it taken me so long? I hadn't always been authentic. I still remember my first husband yelling at me, "Why can't you just be yourself," and realising I didn't really know who my real self was. The study of ontology that I wrote about in *Sizzling at Seventy* helped me become more authentic. Now authenticity was the key to unlocking my heart and though it may have taken a long time to get there, I relish my authenticity. When, following a speaking engagement, people mention how they value my authenticity, I feel that is the highest compliment they can give me.

Becoming an accredited ontological coach will always remain the big game changer for me, but these recent two disciplines – the new look at goals with Mardy and the soul journey with Michelle, were a vital part of my reawakening. I am so grateful for being sent these special women. There were also others too numerous to name but who were of equal importance to me at that time. I felt I was on fire with such a strong sense of purpose and excitement about the future.

My son and daughter are establishing a business in Thailand to support people who are requiring more affordable surgery. Their aim is for a holistic approach to surgery and well being. They have a number of wellness resorts who are keen to be part of the package they plan to offer their clients. One of these resorts offered me four nights complimentary accommodation to trial their facilities. Thanks to my new resolve to make things happen, I put myself forward as a global speaker and offered to speak to staff and guests. My offer was accepted so off I went.

My intuition told me that this was going to be a significant event, but I had no idea that I was going to experience a life-changing process that would be a powerful part of the puzzle of finding my fabulous.

Before I take you to this event, I'd like to introduce a few people to you that have experienced their own grief and come through the other side. They have also found that just because you are fabulous, it doesn't mean that you don't get a few knocks along the way. Being fabulous doesn't make us immune to challenges but overcoming these makes us even more fabulous.

6. LYN'S HEALING TOOLBOX

Sometimes we benefit from a bit of outside help. Before Mick's death, I had felt so self -sufficient. I had done a great deal of work on myself and felt grounded. However, it seems as if there were other things for me to learn. I am thrilled as I look back on the journey and feel extremely grateful for the messengers who helped me get back on track with a new grounding and a strong sense of purpose.

- If it doesn't feel right, don't do it – *'Trust your gut.'*
- Try to remain positive through any trials and tribulations. We don't really appreciate people saying to us, "Everything happens for a reason," especially when we are grieving, but privately I can't help feeling they are right.
- Even when we have found our fabulous, it doesn't mean that we won't get some further knocks along the way.
- I have found that physical pain springs from something deeper. Louise Hay became famous when she wrote *You Can Heal Your Life*. In it, she provided a symptoms list, and when I looked up my symptoms, I had to admit there were some possibilities that I needed to address.
- Believe that this too shall pass. There are so many stories out there about people who have overcome incredible setbacks. Each person has emphasised the need to change their attitude. Changing 'can't' to 'can' is a good first step. Then being open to the next step which may include some kind of intervention. I have found the old saying, "When the student is ready, the master appears," is valid. It means opening ourselves up to a different story. It also means to be detached from the outcome.
- Sometimes we may wonder why a certain situation or person is being presented to us. Follow your intuition, but if you get the feeling there is some purpose to what is happening, you are usually right. We never know what guise our answers appear to us.

CHAPTER 7

Kerri's Story – From Despair Back to Dancing Queen

I mentioned previously in my year of torpor that the one thing I did manage to achieve was to ghostwrite a book about Social Media. One of the best things that happened out of that experience was meeting Kerri Francis. I was looking for someone who had become very successful through networking on social media, and I was referred to Kerri. I began to really enjoy my interactions with her

I loved her exuberance and positivity and was amazed when she told me that she hadn't always been that way. She had experienced many setbacks in her life. The diagnosis of bi-polar brought up more questions than answers, but she was always determined that the diagnosis would not rule her life. This is her story:

Mika scanned the room until his eyes fell upon the beautiful girl dancing wildly in the centre of the room. She flashed a smile at him that seemed to light up the world. He was transfixed by her sparkling eyes and her air of devilment. At that moment he wondered how he could get her to notice him. He felt suddenly rooted to the spot and unable to work out his next steps. Why would someone so amazingly exuberant be interested in a man who was too shy to make a move? He had no idea that he had indeed been noticed. She kept dancing, and her body seemed to glisten with a light he had never seen before. Although she had turned away, unbeknown to him, she had indeed seen him and, as soon as the music stopped, he couldn't believe his eyes as she moved directly towards him. "I'm Kerri, what's your name?" He found himself stumbling over words in his reply. He did not know that she felt an immediate attraction to this tall, handsome man with his smooth, dark skin and bottomless brown eyes. She loved his shy awkwardness and recognised at once that he was the instant, quiet, calming Yin to her bold crazy Yang. She instinctively knew that this was a man who would never try to tame her, and the attraction was strong and immediate.

Within the week they found themselves hopelessly besotted with each other and the thought of being apart was something they could not contemplate. It wasn't long before they moved in together. It was a heady time for them both, and within six months they announced their engagement. Both industrious workers, they managed to put a deposit on a house and worked on plans for the rest of their lives. Like most newly engaged couples, they felt that nothing could dim their love or the certainty of the wondrous life ahead.

Then Kerri found herself pregnant. Sadly, unbeknown to them, this was the point when the magic began to unravel. Kerri found the pregnancy difficult. The heady courting days had left her unprepared for what was happening to her body. She suffered numerous complications that made her feel ill and unable to enjoy what she had anticipated would be a wonderful experience. As her body swelled, every day she longed for a reprieve from the illness that threatened to overwhelm her. What was happening? None of her friends seemed to have these experiences when they were pregnant. She felt that she was losing her mind, not understanding that the combination of physical, social and emotional changes experienced in pregnancy, can cause some people to experience mental health issues, resulting in extreme anxiety and in some cases depression. She began to feel like a failure. It seemed that she was unsuited to pregnancy and she couldn't wait for it to be over. Maybe things would get better.

They welcomed a beautiful baby boy into their world, but the birth did nothing to ease the growing tensions in the relationship. They had so little time to adjust to their love and get to know each other, and now suddenly there was a new baby, new mortgage and now only one income. Kerri longed for her family who had always been there for her but now seemed so far away.

Just when they thought that things couldn't get worse, they did. Mika lost his job which had devastating results. They had been so proud of their plans for the future in their own little house, but now that dream was gone. With Mika's job gone and Kerri unable to work, they couldn't keep up the loan repayments. They were forced to give up their house and declare bankruptcy. The experience left them feeling battered and broken and unable to rationally talk out their problems in a positive way. Living together became so strained they agreed to separate for a while. It was during this time that they found that baby Izacc Francis was autistic. This latest blow was an assault to Kerri's emotional state and she blamed herself, feeling it was all her fault.

Eventually, they worked together to resolve some issues which allowed them to get back together and eventually get married. As responsible parents, they wanted to give Izacc the best possible chance to live a normal life. They sought interventions that could lessen the deficits and problem behaviours associated with (ASD) Autism Spectrum Disorder so that he could gain a quality of life and functional independence. These interventions and therapies bled their dwindling resources dry, and Mika was forced to work three jobs. This left him very little time to interact with his family. This included support for Kerri as she fought to minimise the problems that little Izacc could face by working with the expensive therapies which ultimately proved to be so valuable.

A few years later a second baby boy joined the family, and further pressure was placed on an already fragile marriage. This tested them both and their mental and physical health were compromised. For one thing, it is not easy to be the parent of an autistic child. Any diagnosis causes parents to have to cope with multiple emotions such as grief, worries about the future, and the struggle and expense of obtaining appropriate services to assist the child. There is also the uncertainty about what caused their child's autism and, as in Kerri's case, the guilt – even when it is underserved – about whether it was something they did or didn't do that may have led to their child's ASD (Autism Spectrum Disorder). The stress put on any family under these circumstances can never be overrated.

On top of that, Kerri was feeling repulsed by what she saw in the mirror. She felt no resemblance to the sparkly eyed dancing queen that Mika had fallen in love with. She was overweight, broke and it felt as if bits of her were also broken. This was truth time. She could no longer hold it all together. How could everything that had been so promising go so terribly wrong?

To the outer world she was the same gregarious Kerri, but away from the crowd, standing on her own, afraid to look in the mirror, she realised she couldn't continue living this way. The demons that she had fought to bury began to get the better of her. She had hit rock bottom. It was a hard truth, but it seemed to her that her family would be better off without her. There was nothing more she could do. She shared her feelings of hopelessness with her husband and asked him what he was going to do with the children once she had gone. She was finished, washed up. Her belief in anything that could redeem the situation had completely diminished.

"I don't believe in anything anymore. I'm just not strong enough."

Redemption comes in strange packages, and for Kerri, it began with a phone call from her friend who raved about a new skin and health product she had found. She urged Kerri to come to a party that was going to showcase these amazing new products. Always wanting to support her friends in any enthusiastic pursuit, she feigned excitement for her friend. Underneath she was thinking that she didn't even want to be on this planet, let alone go to a skincare party. She reluctantly agreed to go, knowing that she had no intention of attending.

Kerri left her home that night with every intention of ending her life. It was her darkest hour. She had kissed her babies and man goodbye believing it was time to go, but her persistent friend had other ideas. Again, her friend's phone call interrupted a process she had been determined to follow through. Once more her friend was begging her to come to the party. She felt torn as it was always hard for her to say no to a friend. She reluctantly agreed, still bent on following through on her plan sometime that night.

Kerri found herself at the party after all, and even through the gloom of her shattered mind, she couldn't help reacting to the positive vibe in the room. Everyone was friendly and eager to make her feel welcome. There was lots of hilarity as they tried products and encouraged Kerri to try a wrap that was touted as being able to cleanse toxins and aid in getting rid of belly fat. She was given the spiel:

While many body wraps simply cause water loss, this one uses a botanically based cream formula that, when applied to the skin, gives you tightening, toning and firming results that last. Blah, blah, blah!

She looked down at the body she had grown to hate and secretly thought that this was a load of rubbish. As if a body wrap could do anything with the flab she was carrying. Still, there was no harm in going along with the farce. She was in a very dark and bitter place and was bent on proving that it wouldn't work. She found herself agreeing to take a wrap home to try out, feeling sure that it wouldn't.

The moment she found that it did work was the moment that saved her life because she did feel some instant result and it changed her thought processes. There was a glimmer of hope. The super positive sales lady put a WHAT IF scenario to her. "What if you and Mika could make an income out of this?" Her first mental response, prompted by fear, was to look for an excuse, "HELL NO, I don't have time." But a seed was planted in her mind.

All the way home her feverish brain tried to suppress the possibilities. "What if I could feel better about myself? What if I could help others feel better about themselves? What if I could make money? What if I could have a work-life balance once more?" She began to feel that this was a risk worth taking.

She returned home that night to a distraught husband. Mika had been watching the deterioration of his marriage, his beautiful wife and the life they had tried to create, and he had felt powerless to stop it. Working three jobs and returning to a home filled with tension, left him with no reserves, and now he thought she had gone.

But here she was beside him, and as he lifted his tear-stained face, he noticed something different. There was a small spark of the old Kerri as she put her arms around him and explained that she had listened to an opportunity which she would like to have a go at and something she felt could maybe work. He couldn't believe what he was hearing.

"Babe, I'm going to join the business and give it a go," announced Kerri. Mika rolled his eyes.

"Baby, whatever makes you happy, I'm all for it," he replied. There had been a change in her demeanour, and whatever it was, he would totally support it.

There was no spare money for her to join the company, so she asked her mother if she could please pay for her starter kit.

"I'll never see that money again," commented her mother as she begrudgingly agreed. In that instant, Kerri's torpor was banished, and a spark was ignited.

"I've had enough of people thinking I'm a quitter who never finishes anything," thought Kerri. She reflected that she had spent a lifetime trying to please others but was only ever seen as the black sheep of the family. Others had difficulty in accepting her differences, even when she had tried so hard to be the person that they wanted her to be. It didn't work, and she was left feeling that she could never measure up to their expectations. She decided she was through with being a victim. She was sick of feeling sorry for herself. This was a light bulb moment. "I am the change I need to make in becoming who I really want to be!"

She paid her mother back the next day by pre-selling some products out of her pack. She was determined to prove them wrong.

As is often the case, it wasn't quite that easy. It is a big leap to go from mental instability to being super confident and healthy. It was a constant struggle of worthiness. One day she would be out there rocking the business and the next she would go into a spiral of self-loathing, unable to spend even a minute working on the business. It was a constant struggle for worthiness.

Then something happened that changed everything. She was asked to meet a leader of the company who had recognised the effort she had been making and the great things she was achieving. Kerri fell apart as she told this amazing woman about her struggles and the decision she had made to end her life prior to attending the skincare party. Attending the party had stopped her doing something that would have had such an impact on so many lives. The leader smiled and told her that the company's mission statement was about changing lives.

"I want you to change lives by telling your story at our Sydney conference in two weeks." Kerri was taken aback at the thought of being on a stage, telling her story.

"HELL NO!" was her initial response. She had a life-long fear of crowds. Then that internal voice kicked in. "WHAT IF?"

"What if my story could save someone's life?" she concluded. She felt nauseous as she found herself agreeing to tell her story. Through tears and fear, she stood in front of the crowd and touched all who heard her as she recounted her journey. Very few people knew about her struggles, including her parents, until the clip of her interview went up on YouTube. And then it happened. There was an influx of messages which moved her deeply.

"You have no idea what you have done for me Kerri, I have felt the same and your courage has given me the strength to go on." Could this be possible? Could it be that little old Kerri, who had felt like such a failure had made an impact with her story? It thrilled her that sharing her story had inspired others to keep going. It was then that she had her epiphany. Maybe she had just saved someone's life as hers had been saved – someone's mum, wife, daughter, sister. She knew she had found her calling.

Following the event, she met with Sarah Rankin who was the person above her. In Multi-evel marketing terms, Sarah was her 'upline'. Sarah was incredibly successful and immediately connected with Kerri. She was a small-town girl just like Kerri, and her story was all about failing forward. There was no perfection needed to get there. No fake crap. Just a genuine human, guiding others to greatness.

"Girl, your mess is your message. Own it and go crush goals," advised Sarah. Kerri was moved when Sarah told her she was on her team.

"Alone we are a drop, but together we are the ocean," stated Sarah.

Kerri's head was spinning. She had found her tribe. These were her new friends. They were uplifting, loving, caring people. It was something she loved to be for others but found it hard to be for herself. She had been put down so much in her life and here were people encouraging her and making her feel that she had so much to offer. How was she going to get past her feelings of inadequacy?

Then came the training for her to design her business. They called it 'Mindset Coaching'. She was introduced to the Law of Attraction. This was a new way of thinking for her. Was this all hocus-pocus? Despite her misgivings, she decided that she would give it a go.

So here she was surrounded by incredible people espousing the Law of Attraction and Mindset Coaching. She was beginning to make money and inspiring others with her story – all the while thinking, "Who the hell am I? I'm Kerri version two - the new happy version of myself." And while this was happening, Kerri had lost three dress sizes using the company's products. She was also able to pay a whole month of pre-school fees, taking the stress off her husband. The best thing is that she could do this whilst being at home with her babies.

With all that was happening, before she knew it, her relationship with her family had grown stronger, and they were all noticing a sharp mindset change. Some days were still dark. It is a strange phenomenon that there are those who actually prefer us to be broken. This was certainly the case with some people in her world. They felt challenged by this new Kerri and did what they could to pull her down. It was a huge transition for her to shake off the negativity these former friends brought into her life. Fortunately, the people in her new-found tribe proved to be the light in the dark, and they provided her with the support she needed to pull through.

Kerri feels she is the best version of herself through the incredible support she has received and is now making it her life-long mission to be a light for others. She still practices a mind-set that gets her through each day to reach higher. She states that confidence is the new sexy and imperfections can be attractive. What a revelation that being uniquely her is something she loves being daily.

I was so touched by Kerri's story and love some of the uplifting things she posts on FaceBook to sincerely inspire her team. Some examples of her daily pieces of advice to her loyal team:

"Your value doesn't decrease based on someone's inability to see your worth."

"I'm sick and tired of hearing people give up on themselves because someone else said it wasn't possible!"

"Tell me what in this world does work the same way for absolutely everyone?"

"Don't let others self-limiting beliefs rub off on you!"

"My belief is you're worthy, you're capable, you're powerful and you CAN do the very thing you truly desire!"

"Dare to stand alone and watch life become the greatest blessing you have ever experienced."

After all Kerri and Mika have been through, we only have to look at these two beautiful human beings and their two special children to feel that everything is possible. I was extremely touched by the following Facebook post from two people who almost let something wonderful slip by.

WARNING! SMOOSH POST:

Mika: I've never felt real love until I met you! I never really learnt trust until I met you! I never really knew the meaning of family until we had our own!

Kerri: I LOVE YOU, and I'll continue to shout from the rooftops without fear of retribution for the rest of my waking days.

You have every reason to shout from the rooftops Kerri – you are certainly one fabulous woman and you have an equally fabulous husband. You are both an inspiration to so many.

I would like to add that with them both working in the business together, Mika has created a special venture for himself. He works with children with disabilities, helping them with activities to help their mobility and ability to cope with the general expectations of society. What a beautiful man. Together, these two have not only found their own 'fabulous', they also work daily at helping others to be the best version of themselves. I feel so privileged to have been allowed into their world.

7. KERRI'S HEALING TOOLBOX

- When life gets dark, be open to change. Tomorrow is another day.
- Be willing to take risks.
- Don't listen to the negative assessment of others. Often it is their own stuff running their agenda. Go by your own gut feelings.
- Morning rituals are good. We take turns to pick an inspirational angel card which sets up our day.
- Every day when my children get out of the car, I say, "I love you. Make good choices. Be the best you can be and have the best day ever. Miss you already." They reply with, "Love you more mum. We will. You too."
  I feel it's important to give them repetitive reminders to be good humans.
- Getting your mind right before bed and ending your day with gratitude and love sets the tone for blissful sleep.
- Meditation is a wonderful practice.
- Eating healthy food and exercising helps get your mind right.
- Create a new story for yourself.
- Be okay about having days when you are not okay.
- Release the happy hormones. When you make an effort to be grateful every day, it is amazing how you find the happy hormones flow through you. When you feel down, you double your efforts by using a process that suits you. Gratitude is so powerful.
- The five people in your life that surround you, besides your family, reflect your values. Surround yourself with those that reflect you. If your friends and contacts don't reflect your values, reflect on whether they should be in your life.

CHAPTER 8

No Such Word as Can't

Before I unveil the next exciting experiences of my quest for finding my most fabulous me, I am going to clarify in these next few chapters, that finding your fabulous is not the end of the journey. We can reach some pretty spectacular heights and be really confident that we have found our fabulous, then we can be given another challenge that might rock our foundations. This was my experience following Mick's death and the circumstances surrounding it.

In my previous book, *Sizzling at Seventy*, I wrote a chapter about my son Matt who suffered a horrendous injury as a young child. Considering this book is about finding your fabulous, it is fitting for me to include an update of his story. There was a great deal of grief for a period of time, following his accident, but he certainly showed us how fabulous he was at a young age. I will re-cap the first part of the story for those who have not read '*Sizzling*'.

Matt was always a quiet little kid. Apparently, I had been a very adventurous child, with a range of skills that allowed me to escape from even the highest fences, even managing to take my three-wheel bicycle over a high fence that was supposed to keep me behind bars. I am not sure at what age I remember my mother yelling at me that she hoped one day I would have a child as bad as I was. I think somebody heard her and gave me Simon. Not that Simon was a bad kid at all, just extremely adventurous, as I had been. Not wanting to break his spirit, I tried to prepare myself for each new catastrophe. Whilst Simon was good at Houdini escapades and was a human wrecking ball, Matt would stand back and watch his brother's antics with a mystified air. Mind you, the combined pair managed to get into all sorts of mischief, yet Matt, often in a world of his own, always seemed to be nursing a secret he couldn't share with the rest of us. Together they were adorable, and I loved how protective Simon was of his little brother. They were often seen with their arms around each other and very rarely were there any squabbles. Subsequent events changed the relationship quite drastically.

Matt was not quite seven when he was hit by a car whilst waiting to cross the road. The driver was hugging the curb, and an overhanging bush managed to prevent him from seeing Matt. Consequently, the protruding handle of the old Holden wiped out the side of Matt's head, leaving him with his brain exposed. We were fortunate that a neighbour had called an intensive care ambulance which, because there had been a copious loss of blood, ultimately saved his life. We found out later that the police had found remnants of bone and brain on the door handle and told the driver that there would be no hope for this little boy.

They were not the only ones to proclaim that there was no hope. When my friend raced me to the hospital where the ambulance had taken him, a specialist told me that he had for a short period stopped breathing and, in the unlikely event of him surviving he would most probably be in a vegetative state. At that time, I felt it would be better if he died.

A neurosurgeon was not available at this hospital, so an ambulance was ready waiting to take him to another hospital which was twelve kilometres away. I was instructed to sit in the front of the ambulance and not look as Matt was placed in the back with three paramedics. They felt that I should not witness the sight of my beautiful son with his brain still protruding from his head. These dedicated people were doing the best they could for Matt.

The police tactics stunned me when I noticed them holding back traffic to ensure the ambulance could quickly get through the heavy Easter traffic. I was reminded by the paramedics that this was happening to give Matt the best chance to live. They encouraged me to hold it together. This was difficult when Matt stopped breathing several times and I realised how badly I wanted him to live, no matter what state he was in. The sound of an ambulance siren still has an unsettling effect on me.

We arrived at the Austin hospital, in Melbourne, and I was told to stay in the ambulance until they took Matt out. I was in such a stupor I didn't even think to look, and I can't remember even going into the hospital. I do remember this man coming toward me clothed in what looked like a white boiler suit. He had unruly red hair and a pleasant smile. I thought he was a maintenance man. He shook my hand and told me that he was the surgeon, Dr Woodward, who was going to operate on Matt. He assured me that he would do everything he could, but it was urgent that the brain was covered to prevent bacteria from causing infection.

The next long five hours I was in a daze. At last two doctors approached straight from theatre and proclaimed that a miracle had occurred. Matt had literally died three times, and they had not expected him to survive, but he had, and whilst they had no idea of the prognosis, this was a positive first step.

The next ten days as he lay in a coma in intensive care was an incredible experience. I would talk and sing to him for hours in the hope that he could hear me. He assured me later that he had. We were able to deduce two facts at this time, even though he lay in a coma. The fact that he was still breathing was a miracle in itself, but there were a few things that were evident. We were able to observe him experiencing seizures and secondly when he did have a seizure, his left side was motionless. It was amazing to watch the fluid rushing to protect his brain which was now covered with skin.

His first words, on regaining consciousness a few weeks later, were that he wanted his favourite soft toy which happened to be Woody Woodpecker. He then cried and said he couldn't move and that he wouldn't ever be able to walk. I assured him that everybody was working hard to get him better and now he had to do his part. That was the one, and only time I ever heard him say anything negative about his future. From that day on he worked incessantly on getting better. Before long he was given his own special little walking stick, which we called his 'magic stick'. He practised walking up and down his ward until nurses would stand with tears in their eyes, astounded at his determination. His dear little face drooped down on the left, and his arm dangled helplessly at his side.

Watching him in occupational therapy was a revelation to me. When first asked to draw himself, he drew only his right side. As each day passed, he gradually drew in his left leg, then the foot. It took a while before his arm began to appear, in fact, it didn't make a lot of progress until he left the hospital a few months later.

When he was initially discharged, it was decided to allow nine months at least before his head would be repaired. His brain pulsated at the right side of his head, so I would bandage it firmly each day and place a helmet on to protect it. He continued his daily walking practice, beating the ground with his little fist if he fell. I was not allowed to intervene if he fell over as he insisted on pursuing his practice. I made play dough for him and placed both hands over the dough to encourage movement. One day one finger of his left hand moved ever so slightly, and a big grin broke out on his face. It was the beginning of a long haul to regain movement in his whole hand and arm. The worst aspect of this part of his recovery is that he would have seizures and we were always concerned that he would hurt his head.

A few months later, Dr Woodward felt it might do Matt good to spend a few hours at school. I related this exciting news to him, but he was distressed about wearing his helmet. He knew he couldn't go without his walking stick, but he was really embarrassed about wearing the helmet. I explained that we could not risk leaving his head unprotected and he reluctantly conceded.

As he hobbled along the corridor of the school leaning on his stick, I noticed a tear roll down his cheek and I ached for him. Minutes later, more than one tear coursed down my cheek when I looked through the classroom window and saw every child in the classroom wearing a helmet on their head. What's more, they looked as if it was the most natural thing in the world to be wearing a helmet in class. That wonderful young teacher paved the way for Matt's rehabilitation in the classroom.

Eighteen months later it was time for the head repair to take place and Matt's surgeon explained the dilemma he had. Not many people survive losing half their skull, so he wasn't sure where he would take bone to insert into Matt's head. He told me not to wait at the hospital but to surround myself with friends, and he would let me know as soon as he was finished.

I held my son tightly as the stretcher arrived to take him to the operating theatre. His newly shaved head, exposing the pulsating of his brain through the skin, touched me deeply. I told him how much I loved him, and he grinned at me and assured me that he was coming back.

Five hours later I received a jubilant phone call from Dr Woodward who was really proud of his handiwork. He had taken two of Matt's ribs and grafted them into the side of his head. He explained that ribs grow again, so this seemed the best option. They have proven to be a great success as the ribs in his head have grown and fused together beautifully. What a magnificent feat. We were so fortunate to have Dr Woodward as Matt's surgeon.

Matt recovered amazingly quickly and whilst he did have the occasional seizure, they were far less frequent. The hard part now was rehabilitation. He could read before he went to school and now he had to start from scratch. It took years for him to be able to speak freely and his learning was severely impaired. However, life went on, and he continued to exercise and eventually gained a reasonable power of movement on his left side.

Matt's initial grief was that he couldn't read and that he wouldn't be able to fulfil his dream of playing the guitar. Whilst he understood everything that was spoken to him, he had difficulty in replying. It was almost as if he had to wait for the wheels of speech to begin. Sometimes his inability to reply was misunderstood and a few saw it as rudeness.

Simon's grief was that the boy who returned from the hospital was not the little brother he had adored. There had been a change in Matt's personality that took some adjustment. Sadly, Simon never regained his former close bond with his little brother and recently he related to me that he still grieves for the lost bond.

Matt never at any time gave up. To this day he still exercises his only remaining handicap which is the mobility in his left hand. He seemed to always know the best method to use to rectify any remaining reminders of the accident that almost took his life. In his fourth year at school, he asked if he could learn the trumpet as the left side of his face still drooped and he thought that playing the trumpet would strengthen it, which it did.

I happened to be teaching at the same school he attended for a few years. For some reason, the principal didn't take to Matt, and he complained to me that Matt ignored him when he tried to have a conversation. I explained the difficulty Matt had in answering people, but it didn't seem to make any difference. He was popular with most of the kids and in Year 7 was elected school captain. The principal tried to reverse the decision made by popular choice, but those who voted for Matt held firm. At the end of the year, the principal apologised to me. He had been concerned about Matt's ability to fulfil the duties of his captaincy but was astonished how well Matt went beyond the call of duty in his role as school captain. The principal admitted that he had never witnessed any student be so innovative and dedicated to the role. It wasn't the last time that his abilities were underestimated, but he always soldiered on. He became master of his own race and his ability to not care what anyone thought didn't always serve him.

In high school, he explained to his art teacher that the right side of his brain was extensively damaged, and he would probably never be any good at art. There have been so many creative and compassionate people in his life and here was another. She gave him the book "Drawing on the right side of the brain" a revolutionary book written by Betty Edwards in the seventies. This was before the notion of the brain's ability to regenerate became common knowledge. Matt followed the exercises recommended and practised them. The result was startling. Matt vented his frustrations by producing amazingly large paintings depicting rather disturbing images. So much for his brain injury restricting his creativity.

I do not wish to depict him as a saint. There were many times that he pushed boundaries in his quest for normalcy and he certainly won't die wondering. He found his own way to control his epilepsy and is one person who has found a benefit in cannabis controlling his seizures. Strangely it also appears to bring clarity to him where others may experience something different. Having had the evils of this plant drilled into me, I have to say that I have come to acknowledge that it has many benefits and I certainly can observe that he is more functional with its use.

Before his accident, Matt was on track to becoming a top student, but it became a different story. His brother was academically gifted, and for a time Matt felt inadequate in comparison. There were so many things going on for him, and he now says that he found it difficult to know where he fitted. He dropped out of school and went into hospitality which was a big step in his rehabilitation. The fact that he looked good and, thanks to his mother, exhibited good manners, assisted him in being successful in this role. It also forced him to speak, and his dedication to doing the job properly helped him to rise through the ranks.

In his early twenties, he managed to sire a son who has now provided him with much-loved grandchildren. What began with much consternation has become an absolute blessing.

There were times that he found the use of alcohol gave him the courage to be part of a team and helped him fit in, but there was always the niggling thought that this wasn't his path.

Matt could always vividly remember his three transitions to another world when he actually died. He was eager to tell me about these experiences, but a mother wants to talk about their child living, not dying. I wish I had listened more intently to what he was trying to impart to me because his experiences of 'death' have been significant, and he often longs to go back. It wasn't his time and each time he 'checked out', he was brought back again. I used to watch the monitor beside his bed and could see the fragile hold he still had on life. He always remembered these experiences and has retained a connection with this other world which until recent years was quite confusing for him.

Computer technology became a saviour for him. He took to it very easily, and soon found it was his pathway to the future. It was through his natural ability to adapt to computer technology that he began to realise his path. He became front office manager for a large hotel, and as is his usual way of being, he went far and beyond the call of his brief. It was here that his computer skills took hold and he realised that is where his future lay. His confidence improved as did his abilities and he no longer felt that he was not as good as his brother.

It still astounds me how he was able to change the forecast of a negative future into a productive life – one that defied all expectations. We all thought he was fabulous but being fabulous does not hinder your growth. The next part of his journey almost destroyed him.

8. MATT'S HEALING TOOLBOX 1.

Matt was always looking for more ways to improve the perceived weaknesses resulting from his accident. These are a few rules that he placed on himself.

- Turn "*I can't*" into "*I can*".
- Determine for yourself what is within your capabilities but always push the envelope.
- Find a way around things you find difficult.
- Keep away from people who feel sorry for you.
- Be around people who inspire you to do better.
- Always look for new things to learn and explore.
- Be positive – there is always an answer.
- Have a goal for the future, be clear about what you want and imagine how it feels now that you have it.

CHAPTER 9

Overcoming The Black Dog

Matt was always so positive. Ask him how he was and he'd always reply that he was fantastic, so it came as a huge shock to find that there was a time when he no longer replied that he was fantastic. He feels it is important to tell some of this story as he now sees it as a crucial part of his growth.

When Matt moved to Sydney, he innocently became embroiled in a nightmare. He was somehow accused by the company he was working for, of being a double agent who was leaking company secrets to their software supplier in order to resell their systems.

When he had first joined the company, the Managing Director had been very happy with him, and they maintained a great relationship. Unfortunately, the Managing Director died of a heart attack and the Chairman took over the reins. He was a totally different kettle of fish. His shaved head, thick, black moustache and a light coloured-suit were his trademarks. He was difficult to work with and was totally different from the former Managing Director in his approach to his employees. Without giving too many details, it is enough to get the picture that this was not a man you want as an enemy.

One morning Matt was summoned into the executive office where all of the directors were in attendance. At this stage in his life the black dog of depression was already sniffing at his heels, and although he always took his work seriously, he was no longer comfortable at his workplace. It did not help matters when he was asked to sit in front of the board like a naughty child. Suddenly he was being questioned about incidents that he had not caused or even been aware of. The Chairman was a master at intimidation, and Matt found this barrage of questions very hard to handle. At that time, he was in no state to be assertive or able to stick up for himself, which inadvertently made him appear guilty.

Two days later while he was performing some systems training with a couple of his team members, he was again summoned into the conference room by one of the executives and told he was being made redundant because of cost-cutting. Matt knew full well the real reason was the Chairman's paranoia. He wanted Matt gone rather than take any risk that he might know what was really going on. He was given a payout of only two weeks redundancy and practically pushed out the door. This was a major shock to his system. He had always been well respected in his career until then and had never been in such a position.

It was a very long walk home that afternoon with no laptop in hand, feeling completely lost, alone, rejected and depressed. He had been so excited about relocating to Sydney and had no idea about what he was to face. Little did he know this was only the beginning of one of the worst times of his life. The feeling of hopelessness exacerbated as he slid further into a dark cloud. He was reluctant to tell anybody at that stage, apart from a very close friend who was genuinely trying to help him, but her actions actually had a negative effect.

For three months he was unable to find a job, it was very difficult even looking for one as his vision was blurred most of the time and he could not focus on anything, so the few interviews he did get, he did not come across with his usual confidence. There had been some other significant challenges behind the scenes that had evoked suicidal thoughts which had since intensified. These thoughts led him to a point where he had begun to research how to kill himself without pain.

He finally landed a job out in the west of Sydney for a small systems company. It was very unrewarding work, and at his peak, he could have done it in his sleep. The commute to work required him to take two trains and then walk four kilometres to get to the office which was located in a very unfriendly part of Sydney's west. Each day, he wrestled with the mantra "I want to die, I want to die." playing over and over in his head during his journey to work.

The business owner he worked for was an aggressive Italian. To make matters worse, he had his son working in the business who was supposed to be under Matt's watch. Although he was trying his best, he could feel the attitudes of the directors turning negative and was actually waiting to be sacked. To his surprise, they kept him on after warning him sternly. They felt that he was capable of doing a good job, but they knew something was wrong.

Thankfully, not long after starting this job, he was offered a position with two ex-colleagues from a previous company. They had started their own small hospitality systems, reselling businesses with a senior member who had also been ousted from a company. Matt was thrilled that he was still respected somewhere and about to be given an opportunity. It was with great delight that he resigned from the awful job in the west and things started to look up. He had been proactive in treating his depression by seeing a doctor and a psychologist. He was prescribed anti-depressants which further enhanced his mood, although now he believes that these were only a temporary measure.

His first assignment at his new job was to go to the Philippines with the other guys to assist with the installation of a small hotel group there. As he was feeling a lot better, he stopped taking the anti-depressants. He then met a beautiful woman and formed a relationship which turned out to be the very opposite of what he needed for his mental health. This was when he began to spiral out of control and on his return home, decided to use the suicide methods he had researched. It was distressing that he had come to this point after he had overcome so many hurdles in his life. But, he felt that he had finally reached his limit and just did not want to face another day. He took a day off work and made his way to a party store to hire a helium bottle. Next, he went to the pharmacy to purchase an oxygen mask. He thought he had everything he needed to carry out his plan because he already had a hose.

Once back home, he focused on carrying out his plan. As he began to assemble the equipment that would end his pain, he found that the hose did not fit the mask. Realising that he would need to go to the hardware store for the correct hose, he tried to get up from the couch where he was sitting. However, no matter how hard he tried, and he did really try, he just could not get up. It was as if something or somebody was pulling him back down and would not let him stand up. He remembers screaming, with tears running down his face. "Please let me die, please!" But nothing was getting him up from that couch.

His body felt numb, and he could not move. He stayed on the couch in tears for hours. He realised that it was dark and he was majorly dehydrated from so much crying and not having drunk water for hours. He decided he needed help, so he called the psychologist who gave him the number of a mental health clinic. The cavalier attitude of the person on the phone did not impress him. Not sensing the urgency, this person said they supposed they could come over but made it clear he didn't want to. At this stage, Matt decided to ride it out on his own. He needed all of his resources which had been seriously depleted.

Close friends had tended to drift away, it was as if he was too much trouble. He didn't blame them. After more than a year of struggling, he finally decided that it was up to him to pull himself out of his debilitating depression. Realising that he could not live like this any longer was a defining moment for him. I like to think this is where the old Matt stepped in.

His body shook as he tentatively rose to his feet determined to find a solution. Yearning to be surrounded by nature and fresh air, he strode to his car and found himself heading out of Sydney to The Blue Mountains. His heart pounded in his chest as he made his way to the pinnacle of the mountain. As he stepped out of the car, he was immediately overcome by the breathtaking scene before him. The lush green valley fell away from the steep cliffs and the mountains stood like sentinels against the blue sky. Apart from the occasional eagle soaring above him, he was completely alone in nature.

Making his way to a rock, he determined to stay as long as he needed in order to rid himself of this insidious illness that had gripped him. It had rendered him incapable of moving forward to the rewarding future he had previously envisioned for himself. This was truth time and he knew he could no longer stay in this paralysed existence.

He focused intently on being in this place and visualised pulling this illness out of his head. He now recognises that what he was doing was a form of meditation. It was as if he was standing beside himself looking at the broken form sitting on the rock and seeing clearly what was happening to him. He began to receive affirmative messages that all was not lost. The solitude and the natural beauty of the location helped him to get clarity and to ground himself until he could feel the cloud of depression lift. He felt like he could physically see the depression being pulled out of him. On reflection, he believes he received some form of spiritual assistance which he couldn't identify at that time but has become clearer in the light of subsequent experiences.

It took forty-eight hours before he could feel something happening. It was like there was a clearing of the clouds after many months of storms and he could think clearly again. He didn't really understand what had caused his demise or what was happening at the time, but he left the mountain feeling happy and positive about the future. As his lungs expanded, he experienced a huge breath of fresh air. With his breathing came a new urgency to live. He could feel it throbbing through his veins.

Matt had previously been rather cynical about those who suffered anxiety and depression and had been heard to mutter, "Build a bridge and get over it." Now he reflects that though going through a deep depression is a frightful experience, he believes he came out of it a better human being. He felt more in tune with his own and others' feelings and with a more positive outlook on life. He feels that it actually changed his life for the better which is why this story has its place in his journey.

9. MATT'S HEALING TOOLBOX

Matt had overcome so much and tended to be impatient with those who suffered anxiety and depression. He is now glad that he understands that where our mental health is involved, we can't just snap our fingers and be over it.

- Learn to trust your intuition – if it doesn't feel right, don't do it.
- Be patient with yourself and don't be ashamed to seek help.
- Stay away from negative people.
- Surround yourself with positive people who uplift you.
- Transmute your grief into something positive such as exercise.
- Get out of the house and ground yourself in nature, walk barefoot on the beach or a grassy park.
- Think of things that you love and make you happy.
- Take the opportunity to laugh as much as you can, watch comedies or be around people that make you laugh.
- If you feel up to it, make a list of everything you have achieved.
- Monitor your language and keep telling yourself: You CAN do this.
- The most important message is that even at our worst moments, we have no idea what is ahead. We have to hang in there as the tide always turns.

CHAPTER 10

Finding His Tribe

Not long after his recovery, Matt was given the opportunity to become a regional Hotel Services Manager for a remote site services company serving the oil industry in Kazakhstan. It was a new experience to be in charge of 700 employees, most of whom knew very little or no English. He managed to achieve much with a band of devoted employees. I often wonder if it was his own struggles that assisted him to become such a good manager. However, it was when his skills in technology became known, he found himself much in demand. I also believe his return to his former optimism, following his horrific experience, helped everything else to fall into place.

Following his enjoyable two years in Kazakhstan, he often regretted that he heeded a call from a company in Dubai which turned out to be another stressful period of his working life. The shallow glitz of Dubai did not compensate for how badly he was treated at his workplace. It was a relief when after two years he was offered a job in Nigeria. Whilst Nigeria is not always a safe place to be, he found his year there a blessed relief and enjoyed working with a professional, friendly staff.

He really enjoyed his next role which was a nine-month contract as Senior Project Director for Ascot Hotels. This was a global project that involved 117 businesses in 17 countries. How far he had come from the teenager, who had been told that he would never succeed in hospitality. It was never envisioned that he would reach this level. He had gained so many skills, and there was no doubt that he demonstrated the plasticity of the brain.

With his burgeoning knowledge about computer data and systems programming, for several years he had been developing an innovative new system which could be used to manage remote site services. This included accommodation, travel and stock control. Whilst in Dubai, he had started a company with a business partner. They felt the time was right to launch full-time into the business and it was decided to start a development hub in Manilla. He was very excited and found an office space which he painted in bright colours. Unfortunately, he was about to face another hurdle and another stressful period of his life.

At the time I was coping with Mick's death, Matt was experiencing the imploding of his dream. He had poured his resources into his business and was now experiencing a lack of funds. It was at this time he met his present wife, Beverly and instantly fell in love. The problem was that Bev had been contracted to work in Dubai and was about to fly out there. In his already stressed state, he begged her not to go. Beverly felt that she must honour her contract and left as planned. Matt decided to fly to Dubai to attempt to bring her back. It was no easy task as he found that workers from the Philippines were exploited and given tight contracts. However, his determination to bring her home prevailed and after a lot of difficulties he succeeded.

Neither of us can remember how or why I arrived in Manilla a few weeks after Mick's death. My memory is that he asked me to come, but it is still a mystery how I came to be there. Neither of us was in a very stable state, so it was like the blind leading the blind. It was lovely to meet Bev, and I was thrilled when they were married a few months later.

Matt, finding the stress of the business beyond his expectations, sold his share to his partner and took up a contract with a company in Gabon, West Africa, as their IT director. The contract was initially supposed to be short term but somehow the time stretched to five years which meant six weeks in Gabon and three weeks in Manilla with Bev. As the project was winding down, he was able to manage the IT position remotely and decided to take up my offer to come and stay with me in Australia. Bev had stayed with me several times over the previous years, but now it was the big move to another country.

Over the years Matt met so many people and had successfully carved out a career far beyond the expectations of many naysayers, but there was still something missing. He really hadn't found his tribe. Apart from his long-term friend Dave, he hadn't found a group of people that he could totally relate to or who he felt he could share the spirituality, which had become so much part of his life since his experience on the mountain top.

I believe that everything happens when the time is right – divine timing – and it seemed that Matt had to come to Australia where he had time and space to look deeper into his soul and get the guidance he needed for the next part of his journey.

Several years ago, I went with Matt and Bev to a meditation session at the beach conducted by the gifted medium, Jason McDonald. During the meditation, Jason told Matt that he was a Shaman and should follow this calling. This resonated with Matt. It wasn't the first time he had been given this message, but the time was right for him to explore. He did some research and found out about Kevin Turner who taught core Shamanism in seven different countries. He felt moved to sign up for the next course which was to be in Bali the following year. It seemed a natural next step to his life. Reading Kevin's experiences, such as the one below recorded by Kevin, mirrored so many of his own.

"As early as I can remember I experienced nocturnal journeys to an attic above the attic to learn from ancestors, or to a cellar below the cellar that led down to fairy-tale realms. Unable to distinguish the difference between waking, lucid dreaming or otherwise in these worlds, I rarely spoke of them or the things I learned.

When I learned shamanic journeying from Michael Harner, I immediately realized what had been occurring since childhood, but now I had a framework within which to work. It was an awe-inspiring development in my life, and it's an honour to be able to share this with others as an FSS (Facility Support Services) faculty member in Asia."

I had known about shamanism for many years but have to confess I had never gone to the trouble to find out much about it, until that time. I found that it is perhaps the oldest system without any scriptures or dogma, that entails man seeking connection with creation. With shamanism, you don't have to share the same beliefs as another. It is more concerned about why things happen in our lives and what might be going on beneath the surface of things. It is concerned with why and how we came to be.

I loved the notion that shamanism is concerned with the natural flow of life and nature. It teaches respect for all fellow creatures and with each other. The more I read about it, the more I resonated with the good that it inspires, though it is often misunderstood. I read Kevin Turner's book, "Sky Shamans of Mongolia" and was enthralled with the history and rituals of the work done in Mongolia by Shamans. (See reference section)

I like this quote from Brett Almond, 'Beginners Guide to Shamanism'
Shamanism is something with which you feel a connection. It is not something to which you sign up. It is not about having powers, but it is about the power to be ourselves, to live the way we would like to live and to feel connected to something greater than ourselves.

There was a difference in Matt even following his first workshop with Kevin. He knew he had found his tribe and the practices he was learning were already familiar to him. He also understood why the journey had been so challenging at times.

I was moved when he offered me a healing session. Was this really my son who had experienced so much? The son that I had been told would never be able to amount to anything and could possibly be a vegetable for the rest of his life. Here he was with his drum and so capably performing these ancient rituals as if he had been doing them all his life. I was incredibly moved and felt an immediate sense of peace. He was able to pick the places in my body that needed healing and over the following weeks, I could feel changes.

Now with his advanced training in shamanism, he continues to use his skills to help others. Each time he learns more and becomes more in tune with his helping spirits.

We never know what experiences lay ahead and just because we find our 'fabulous', it doesn't mean that there are no more mountains to climb, but the climb is always worth it.

I have included Matt's story because it demonstrates that we can have many experiences that make us feel that we have reached the pinnacle of 'fabulousness', but then suddenly we may feel it whipped away from us. Matt had overcome so much since his accident, but he still needed to learn more, and whether we can relate to his story or not, the fact is that he is thankful for the lessons that have brought him to a place of peace and wisdom. He also cherishes that he now is developing skills that assist him to help others.

10. MATT'S HEALING TOOLBOX

As I have been writing Matt's story, it has reminded me how little we really know about our children. There was so much going on in Matt's life that I really did not know about and I think he has shown a great deal of strength in overcoming a number of obstacles.

Some suggestions from Matt:

- Don't be discouraged by anybody telling you that you can't do something.
- Look to the end result of what you want. If you visualise this frequently, the path will unfold.
- Most importantly; don't put any limits on yourself. We are capable of achieving anything that we put our minds to.
- Stay positive and go for it.
- We are all here with a purpose. It is possible to find that purpose through meditation and being in tune with what you are being led to do.
- Be open to anything that life puts before you, then use your intuition to know whether this is a path for you.

CHAPTER 11

Finding My Own Fabulous

N ow back to my story.

I had no expectations about my trip to Phuket, in Thailand. In my newly constructed cloak of invincibility, I decided I was going to throw myself into everything. I believed I would be given the strength I needed to do whatever task I was given. Ha, ha; here was another lesson I needed to learn. I was reminded that along with invincibility there needs to be a little dob of prudence.

The resort was quite a drive from Phuket Airport, made longer by the many roadworks and a driver who could not speak English. I enjoyed taking in the sights and sounds along the way but was relieved when we turned into a street lined with interesting looking dwellings, quite different from the street scenes. Although the architecture was still distinctly Thai, it was obvious that the area was inhabited by the well-heeled.

We turned into a long drive that was dotted with little thatch-roofed villas that are unique in Thailand. We eventually stopped at the main building where I was greeted by friendly smiles, a delicious, healthy drink and a cooling towel which made me aware of the driblets of perspiration running down my back. A tall, rangy young woman introduced herself in a rather guttural accent and showed me to my room. It was beautifully set up and very cool. The room led out onto a balcony from which there were views of mountains and lots of native fauna. Beautiful birds seemed impervious to the heat as they flew amongst the trees carolling joyfully. I took a deep breath and decided that there were worse places to spend five days.

I knew that the meals were all plant-based, but another delightful surprise was the quality and variety of food served throughout my stay. There was always a theme from another country. Apart from a small selection of local fish, and eggs, served to your taste at breakfast, the food was strictly vegan. Every meal was absolutely delicious and was served on a beautifully decorated long table. One night we had dinner served outside and ate by the light of candles and lanterns. I envisioned myself leaving there so much healthier and maybe even thinner.

After lunch, I was approached by a vision of splendour, decked out in the latest gym wear, which did nothing to hide her fit young body. She introduced herself as Maria Curtin, and I detected an Irish accent. She sat down with me to develop a plan for my time at Phuket Cleanse. As we went through the schedule for each day, I thought to myself, *I can do that!* without taking into account that it had not been long since I had recovered from my year of being in a severely handicapped state. I had only just got to the point of being able to go for half hour walks.

Maria advised me that the walk the next morning was a fairly easy one. We were to be driven to a destination from which we would walk to a bluff to watch the sunrise. My heart sank when I saw the steep rocky track that confronted me. I was determined to do it, and as the others belted down the track, I tentatively stepped down and immediately skidded onto my backside. This was not looking good. One of the young women looked around, saw my plight and hurried back to me. I would have been better with a stick, but she provided an arm to steady me. It was hard going, and when we were three-quarters of the way, I decided to stop and view the sunrise from that spot. I encouraged my human walking stick to go on and, like a released caged animal, she sprang into action, quickly catching up with the others. The sunrise was spectacular, but as I sat there, I thought of the mortification of getting back up the hill. Thankfully, it was so much easier than my downward journey. I was feeling pretty chuffed as I sat waiting at the top for the others, but my pride soon dwindled as the herd came running up the track not far behind me. Tongue-in-cheek, I told my human walking stick that I just couldn't keep helping her all the time and she just had to go it alone.

Following breakfast, I was enrolled in a stretch class which was more in line with my skills, although still quite challenging. My Irish beauty had me stretching inside out, and it felt good. For a bit of reprieve, I attended a talk before lunch, reminiscent of an Anthony Robins style content, conducted by another special young woman. After lunch, I had a swim and then was allocated a tough Thai woman who came to my room and gave me a high-impact Thai massage. I like a firm massage and can endure the pain that comes with it, but this one had me 'ouching' as my body was contorted into shapes I didn't think were possible. My only consolation was convincing myself how wonderful I was ultimately going to feel.

But here came the crunch. For the previous two days, I had been deprived of coffee, alcohol or any hint of sugar and I was wondering why I was feeling so wretched. The evening I was to give my talk, I lay on my bed wishing I didn't have to get up. I felt in no fit state to be able to give of my best. The mirror reflected a swollen and blotchy face with bloodshot eyes. My plan to have my talk filmed had to be abolished, but the show must go on.

When I arrived at the room where I was to speak, it was already full. Sadly, some had to be turned away as there was not even a piece of floor left. I had been given a new opportunity, and I was not going to let a bit of detoxing get in the way. I sallied forth, and before long realised not only was I having a ball, my audience also seemed captivated. It was heartening to see that the majority of my audience were young people in their twenties and thirties and they all felt they had gained something from my talk. The next morning, I found little notes placed in an envelope for me. They were heartwarming. I have enclosed a couple here:

"Lyn, so nice to see such a wonderful, smiling, positive person like you. You are a really strong person. Thank you for the open, beautiful talk. Thank you for being real and showing us all that we have the power to change our lives."

"So lovely to meet you – thank you for sharing yourself and your story with such heart and vulnerability. I warmed to you instantly and can't wait to read the next book."

"To the lady Lyn. It has been an absolute privilege to have met you this week. I feel like it has been fate. Your zest for life and determination has inspired me so much. I look forward to finishing your book and reading the next. I also look forward to meeting up with you in Australia."

It was gratifying to be asked back. If I do go back, I will be smuggling in some coffee. I did enjoy the gentle shamanic meditation that followed my talk. I think I went to sleep.

Prudence may have come late, but I decided to scale back some of the more strenuous activities while still having walks on the beach, stretching and breathing. It was all very wonderful, but at that stage, I had no idea what was ahead, or that I was about to have a life-changing experience.

I am so grateful for all of the lessons learnt in my life. The hardest one for me has been learning to love and value myself, and over the years every bit of work I have done on myself has brought me closer to becoming a true believer. It is crazy that the insults hurled at me as a child and teenager, still sometimes managed to sneak their way into my heart. I worked very hard to prove myself, and when my first book was published almost twenty years ago, my father said, "I bask in your reflected glory but don't tell your sisters, or they will feel inferior." This caused me to feel guilty whenever I had a book published or wrote a play, but I have to say that it didn't stop me trying. Despite my efforts, I was still not feeling very *fabulous*.

I have been learning a lot about lateral violence, mainly in Indigenous communities, where you are punished and bullied if you dare to rise above your station. I now recognise that this issue is not limited to Indigenous communities and in some ways, I experienced it a little of that myself. Low self-esteem is certainly a contributor and a difficult one to deal with.

My recent work with Mardy and Michelle had certainly reignited my efforts, and there were moments when I thought I had eradicated any lingering doubts of my worth, but I found out that I still had a little way to go. What happened next may seem implausible, but it was a very real experience, and it has changed everything for me.

On the third day of my stay at Phuket Cleanse, I enrolled myself in two sessions of re-birthing. It has always been something that has interested me. My older son Simon had a very difficult birth and was not breathing when he was born. I have always felt that his birth may have been a contributor to some of the health and emotional difficulties he has experienced. So, I thought I would find out about the process. What I found was that these sessions were the next important step in my search for my fabulous.

Dela Catudel slid into my room, a vision of ethereal beauty and grace. She took one look at me and pronounced that my throat was blocked and that I still hadn't reached total confidence in myself. Wow, let's get right to it! Her instincts were correct on both counts. I was intrigued by the process she planned to use. I knew it involved breath work but couldn't see how that was going to unblock my throat or give me the last nudge to finding my fabulous.

She sat cross-legged on my bed, her long blonde hair tied back in a ponytail. I was captivated by her finely chiselled features and aura of complete confidence. There was something otherworldly about her. I trusted her immediately and was keen to get going. Dela explained the process which entailed special uninterrupted breathing. I had absolutely no expectations but decided to do as instructed. The process was much harder than it sounded. I found it quite exhausting, and Dela kept urging me on, getting me back in rhythm when I tended to slow down. About 30 minutes into the process I found my throat choking up and felt the need to get rid of whatever was blocking it. Dela instructed me to spit it into the towel she was holding. This happened three times. I had never been able to expectorate, yet here I was hawking like it was an everyday occurrence. I was bringing up lots of 'stuff', and Dela kept encouraging me with words like, "Well done Lyn, keep going".

I am not sure how much time went by before the next major development occurred. In my book, *Sizzling at Seventy*, I spent quite a bit of time explaining the abuse I suffered at the hands of my mother. I very rarely saw her smile and laughter was something quite foreign to her, so what happened next was remarkable and totally unexpected. I was finding the process difficult and wanted to stop, but Dela encouraged me to keep going. Suddenly my mother appeared in very bright colours. I still remember the dress she was wearing in vivid reds and yellow. I recognised her by her very large nose, but now she was smiling, and as she came to me, she placed a large heart shape over my heart. I felt myself smiling and feeling emotional. I didn't want her to go away, but she moved to my side and began pulling something out of me. I found it quite frightening as she seemed to be pulling out my entrails. She was pulling, pulling, pulling and apparently my face froze in a mask of fear. I had no idea what was happening. This process seemed to go on and on but then she returned to me with a smile and placed the shiny heart back on my heart. It is hard to describe how I was feeling. I did feel a little confused, but I also felt very light. It took only a few more minutes for me to come back to the present and open my eyes. Dela checked if I was okay.

"Wow, your mother was really busy. Usually, I have to help this process, but she wanted to do it all," informed Dela. I was stunned. I hadn't mentioned my mother at any time, and no words had been spoken, so how did she know that I had this encounter with my mother.

"Do you know what she was doing?" asked Dela. I shook my head.

"She was pulling out the programming she put into you as a child." This information was mind-blowing, and I reflected that it did look like my mother had been pulling out some kind of tape and I had already checked that my entrails were still safely locked inside my body.

My mother had indeed planted some very negative programming in me as a child, "You are stupid. You are ugly – no decent man will ever want you. You are clumsy, a nuisance ..." and on and on. My father was not a lot better and if they were preventing me from getting a swollen head, they certainly succeeded. I felt that my mother had hated me, yet here she was showing me incredible love and encouraging me to believe that all of the old conditioning had been completely eradicated. This experience made me feel completely depleted but gloriously happy. I also thanked her for the contract we had made for her to teach me so much. My childhood was extremely difficult but navigating it has made me stronger, and now she had set me free.

Dela explained to me that by using the circular breath, without pausing between the inhale and the exhale, an energy flow is created in the body. This flow helps release negative emotions which are stored in the cellular memory of the body. As these emotions become integrated and you keep the breathing and energy flow, you can go to a deeper level and experience profound clarity and a new understanding about yourself. It is not uncommon that the person breathing can experience clarity around some issue that they may have been dealing with. This had certainly happened to me. It was totally unexpected, and however this experience manifested, it has changed everything for me. The last piece of self-doubt has gone, and I am even more ready to acknowledge my own fabulous.

I decided to have another session the following day, and it was equally remarkable, but this next experience was intensely personal, and I am still digesting it. My mother did appear again, this time with a basket of gold stars which she proceeded to throw in the air. She was still in the bright clothes of the day before, and I was so glad to see her. It did involve being told by special people surrounding her, "You can do it, Lyn. You can do it." I was also assured that I would never be alone, and I know I never will be. At the time I wasn't sure what it was that I could do, but the next piece of the puzzle was about to be unveiled.

#11. LYN'S HEALING TOOLBOX

It is exciting to know that just when you think you've experienced everything, something new can be presented. Over the years I have always been open to new learning, and everything that I have done has given me a new little piece of the puzzle. It almost seems as if I have been drip-fed and left to wonder what's next. I have not accepted everything that I have learnt. There have been some things that I have had to ponder and have decided they were not for me, but I was glad of the experience.

- Embrace new experiences. Sometimes we sabotage our growth by denying ourselves new learning. Have an open heart.
- Honour your own contributions without denigrating others. I was not doing my sisters any favours by feeling guilty when I achieved success.
- I still find value in lists. With self-esteem issues, it can be valuable to write down all of your strengths. When you have written all you can think of, have a trusted friend help you add to the list. I used to find this so difficult. Get to know yourself.
- What are the factors that you can identify that contribute to your lack of self-esteem? Mine stemmed from ingrained mantras from my childhood which I kept re-enforcing by attracting the wrong people to me. Once you have identified the markers, ask for a way that you can set yourself free. You can do this in meditations or simply just by asking. Your answer may come in a form that you least expect, but if you ask with a knowledge you will receive, your faith will be rewarded. It is a relief, at last, to be able to let it all go and to be able to value myself in a new light. In my early years, it didn't occur to me to find a way out of my low self-esteem. I just thought it was part of my legacy. What a gift to know that it is possible to learn to value our true worth.
- Know with certainty that we are being helped and supported from a number of sources.

CHAPTER 12

The Next Piece of the Puzzle

Some weeks later, I was still enthralled with the unexpected outcome of my re-birthing experiences. They were still very clear, and I cannot deny the difference it made. I had no idea what was still ahead for me, but I found myself being open to the next part of my journey. There was a clarity that I hadn't experienced before, and I felt a sense of rejuvenation.

My experience in Thailand prompted me to reflect on what had changed in my life and how very close I came to giving up on the notion of fulfilling a purpose or indeed ever really finding what I felt was my own fabulous. It has been good to reflect on the journey of my life and honour my successes. We all have something to offer and at last, I can recognise that I no longer have to doubt what I have to offer but am grateful that it hasn't come easily. I feel that my life experiences have equipped me to do my greatest work and I can do it now with a completely open heart.

I still have to be reminded at times that I have some negative language that has become habitual and I have given my children permission to point out if I make statements such as; *"I'm so stupid,"* when I can't find my glasses or can't think of a name. I have daily reminders, examples of how our thoughts and speech create our reality and revisit my vision board regularly. I'm not at all afraid of death, but I know there is still much for me to do in this life and at last I am in the right space to do it.

Josephine Cashman

A few days after I returned from Thailand, I had a communication from Josephine Cashman, an amazing Aboriginal woman, whom I have coached on and off for seven years. We met when we were both working with an Indigenous company and I was immediately drawn to her. She was beautiful and sassy, but there were moments that I observed her demonstrating quite deep anger around her heritage. Her life story will be told one day as she has been on a unique journey which has seen her rise above many negative experiences.

When Josephine was in a refuge centre, she made a decision to study law. Against all the odds and with little education, she became a brilliant lawyer. Her experiences have led her to be passionate about the effect of domestic violence on communities, and she has focused on this issue in her law practice as well as the work she continues to do in communities.

One case became the subject of an SBS documentary when she successfully prosecuted a man who had subjected his partner to extreme physical and sexual violence which almost caused her to lose her life. It came as a shock to Josephine when, in the first trial of the perpetrator, his defence barrister suggested that domestic violence was accepted within the Indigenous community and even questioned whether this was even a matter for the court. Those who have a real understanding of Aboriginal culture know that this is far from the truth and Josephine continues to dedicate herself to educating others about the real stories surrounding Aboriginal culture.

Ever since I have known her, Josephine's desire has been to assist Indigenous people to be motivated to get out of victimhood and off welfare. She created a foundation called Big River Impact Foundation and gathered a board of powerful people together who believe in her vision and have assisted her in refining it. The mission is dedicated to developing business capability, economic sustainability and financial independence for Indigenous Australians through social-impact investment strategies that deliver far-reaching economic and social benefits. I am blown away by her incredible intellect and innovative vision. I'm thrilled to be asked to play some role in this work.

Previously I have recounted my belief in miracles and I am watching one unveiling before my very eyes. Becoming immersed in this work, Josephine is being taught and led by true spiritual Aboriginal leaders who see the huge role she has to play in bridging the great divide between cultures. We have so much we can learn from this ancient culture and they want so much to share. Josephine is on an important mission and her anger is now gone. She is stepping into a beautiful leadership role and the change in her persona is thrilling to see.

I love these words from Josephine which highlight where she has found herself:

"We are our masters. We choose to be driven by our feelings: happy, sad, jealous or angry, and to allow others, or our environment, dictate our sense of self. Lyn taught me you can rise above emotions. It is a moment to moment choice. We can transcend past resentments even when we have been hurt, abused or hard done by. Some say we do not choose to be born. I disagree. We are divine. Some believe hardship will kill. Abuse is mostly an excuse for bad behaviour by those who do not want to take responsibility.

Pain must be embraced as part of our humanness. Happiness can never be forever. Deflation of fantasy creates hopelessness. I have learned to love hard times and embrace them as a gift. It became possible after I worked through my pain, blame and bitterness. It is liberating. With this mindset, we attract everything we need.

Unconditional love is the key. I am fortunate to be a first Australian. My spiritual elders across our wondrous land describe the role of Indigenous people as the global grandparents."

I have worked with Indigenous groups before, but I have never seen such a holistic approach. I have always believed in this young woman and now I am seeing her dream beginning to flower.

So, I attended a meeting with Josephine which changed my own vision of the future. I have always been passionate in my desire to do what I could in this domain but often felt helpless. I left the meeting with a possible new role to co-design with Aboriginal leaders, an approach to work with Indigenous leaders in communities. Their knowledge is profound but often they feel that their lack of education holds them back and their wisdom is often ignored. They have answers to many of our environmental problems and it would be to our advantage if their voice could be heard. Somehow, I would like to be a part of working with them to help bring this about. At the moment we are not sure what this looks like, but I am sure it will happen.

Once I would have felt daunted, but now I know this is where I am meant to be. Acknowledging my fabulous has turned out to be a far different paradigm than I could ever have envisioned. Maybe, I could have chosen an easier path but it is the one that I have been guided to, and now I know what was meant when I was told, "You can do it, Lyn. You can do it." There is no other time in my life that I would have been ready and everything that has happened in my life, my grief, my pain, my joy, my love, has given me skills I need for the next part of my journey. I now know we have always been fabulous, we just have to recognise our fabulousness. As we do this the rainbow behind the cobwebs becomes more visible.

#12. LYN'S HEALING TOOLBOX

Time for us to recognise how fabulous we already are.

- Make an in-depth and honest list of everything you have done in your life. This includes things like when you helped a neighbour or saved a dog from being abused. Absolutely everything you can think of. You may need someone to prompt you.
- Be open to what's next.
- From your list make some positive comments about the person that you are. "I am kind-hearted." "I care about animals." "I take care of myself." etc.
- Make a careful note of any negative feelings you have about yourself. Are they really factual or are they part of a story you have made up about yourself without realising it?
- Make a list of things you would like to do that would enrich your life. The mood of 'wonder' is useful for this exercise.
- Watch the language you say about yourself.
- Be sure to acknowledge your fabulousness!

CHAPTER 13

The Journey

When I wrote *Sizzling at Seventy*, I thought I had found the end of the rainbow. I recounted the horror of my childhood, my escape into an abusive marriage, my struggles to find myself and the people who helped me. I don't call any of the things that happened mistakes because out of each experience, I gained knowledge. I am full of gratitude that something in me wouldn't allow me to give up.

Studying to be an ontological coach allowed me to become a better observer of myself and others. This was life changing and set me on a more positive path which led me to my beloved husband, Mick. He believed in me and saw something in me that I couldn't see myself. This was new to me as I had previously attracted men who had made it their habit to put me down and I often found myself playing small. They were all part of my journey, and I see that so clearly now.

At the time before *Sizzling at Seventy* was published, I was blissfully happy and saw the partnership with my husband lasting many years. We had so many exciting plans on how we were going to share our future together. Only two months after the book was published, he passed away with an aggressive brain tumour and my world was shattered.

In this book, I have shared the next stage that has also been an important part of my journey. I still miss Mick very much and often feel him near. I ask him questions and still feel his guiding hand. He will always remain a special part of my life.

For thirty years, meditation and prayer have been an important part of my daily routine, but since my recent experience of re-birthing, I am enjoying my daily practice much more. I believe that it is one of the most important practices we can have. I was so excited when a young man I had been coaching, began meditating and it is making a big difference in his being able to handle his anxiety. He finds some of the apps that are available have been an enormous help to him.

I hear so many people say that they just can't meditate. Some find themselves unable to give themselves permission to take the time. My own monkey mind goes into over drive at times, but I was comforted when the Dalai Llama said that he also has days like that. It is called meditation practice for that reason. It is a practice that gets better the more we do it. There are also gurus who tell you that you must do it this way or that and sometimes we feel that we have failed because we don't follow a prescriptive method. I have come to believe that we have to find what works for us. Some benefit from guided meditations, others work with the Chakras etc. There are so many ways that we can meditate.

I find a blend of everything works for me and now I cherish rising early and having that special morning ritual. I find it beneficial to spend a bit of time in stillness. There is a crystal hanging outside my window and as the sun rises, prisms dance around the room. As I observe this dance, I see the light gradually coming into the room causing sentimental objects to be highlighted. This thrills me every time and I am overcome with immense gratitude. A great way to start the day. There was a time that I felt there was nothing to be grateful for. I now know with that frame of mind, there will be nothing that will reveal itself, yet there is always something to be grateful for. I learnt, in the early days of my grief, to consciously look for things for which I could be grateful and was surprised that there were so many. This is now part of my daily practice and if I am tempted to feel depressed, finding so much to be grateful for makes my heart sing.

I have to confess that in my year of chronic pain, I struggled with my daily practice and know that is the time I needed to double my efforts. When I pleaded for help, I began to attract the right people in my life. I began to consciously feel my body healing and would be grateful as it began to get stronger.

It was almost like starting from scratch again, getting down to grassroots with Mardy. First of all, really digging in to acknowledge my strengths with Mardy urging me on. This is sometimes the hardest thing for people of my era to do. We were always told that we must be humble and not think too highly of ourselves. I was a bit surprised that my list was longer than I thought it would be. Then we looked at my perceived weaknesses which allowed me to look at what was holding me back. It was powerful. Then we tackled the specific goals I needed to work towards. Gradually I could feel my confidence returning much stronger than it had before. Catherine, another strong woman, was someone I always admired. Together, these women shocked me out of playing small. Previously when someone remarked that I had a lot of books published, I would say, "But they are only ...." They insisted that I be proud that I have thirty published works and that there is no need to qualify. At last, I feel proud of my achievements. It is okay to feel proud, I declare to my shadow self.

The next step was to open my heart which I had been carefully shielding. I really believe that when the student is ready, the master appears. For this task, Michelle came into my life, and because I was ready, it happened quite quickly.

The re-birthing sessions were the next step for me. Finally removing the programming of 'not good enough' was timely. Once again, I believe I had to spend time in this life, struggling for self-esteem. It has equipped me so well to understand how to help others become their best selves.

I don't think for a minute that from now on there will always be calm seas. Our learning never ends. I feel better equipped to navigate the stormy seas and some hostility that I am bound to encounter. There have been moments when I think about what life would be like just sitting reading and meeting up for coffee. As appealing as it sounds, I do hope I can fit some of that in, but I know that in time I would be sick of that way of life. I prefer to continue working in a purposeful role until I die.

13. LYN'S HEALING TOOLBOX

I hadn't realised that as a child I had learned to shield my heart. Whilst experiencing a particularly difficult time in her life, my lovely granddaughter told me that she was going to put her heart in a box and keep it safe. I realised that is what I had done and bringing it out of the box has not always been easy. I am now more aware that opening my heart is a holistic exercise and am continually learning to be mindful of this.

- Deep breathing has helped me to open my heart. I need to make sure that as I do this, I direct my attention to my heart and put my energy there. I find as I rest there, old energy patterns can dissipate. There are also Yoga poses that can help – Cobra, Upward Facing Dog, Fish pose and others.
- Recently I attended a 'Deep Desire Day' with the lovely Louise Geary. (See reference section.) Louise skillfully assisted the group to tease out the real desire's we have. When I stated mine, I felt the old resistance and Louise picked it up and encouraged me to use an anchor to pull myself out of the hint of the old paradigm returning.
- Practice being truly compassionate with yourself and others.
- Being grateful – some find a gratitude diary reminds them of all they have to feel grateful for. I can now feel grateful for the experiences that seemed so negative.
- A daily practice to suit my needs has helped me to open my heart. It also clears the rubbish out of my brain and mind.
- I've said this so many times, but please be kind to yourselves. I have found that opening my heart has given me more vitality and inspiration. I believe it also helps me to be more authentic in my connections with others.
- No harm will come to you. You are safe to take your heart out of the box and live more freely.
- Breathe, breathe, breathe!

CHAPTER 14

Finding Beauty in Imperfection

We experience grief in so many ways, and we cannot always understand the suffering that may be happening in someone else's life. That is one of the reasons I wanted to include stories from others who have suffered grief that has threatened to wreck their lives and prevent them from finding their true purpose. I am so grateful for those who trusted me enough to allow me to use parts of their story.

I met Tatia Power when my Mick was still alive and at that time we had no idea what was ahead for us. Tatia gave me the opportunity to speak at a networking group in Brisbane. I loved the sound of her voice on the phone and looked forward to meeting her. I felt a bond with her right from the beginning and was glad to meet her in person. What I found was a delightfully exuberant young woman with a genuinely lovely smile. I always know that when I feel this way that I am dealing with authenticity, which is a precious attribute in my books.

I would have liked to spend more time with her and have enjoyed seeing her posts on Facebook. I was delighted when she began sharing beautifully written blogs under the interesting title of *Chasing Enso*. My curiosity led me to look for its meaning, and I was intrigued when I read that in Zen, Enso is a circle drawn in one or two uninterrupted brushstrokes to express a moment when the mind is free to let the body create. It's about finding beauty in imperfection. Tatia's blogs allowed us into her world to reveal deep grief which has dogged her for as long as she can remember. With her permission, I will borrow heavily from her blogs in an attempt to do justice to her moving story. She has so much ability to write with deep feeling, I certainly hope that one day she will write her own book. In the mean-time, I am grateful to her for allowing me to share a small part of her experience.

Tatia can't really recall when she started feeling unworthy of love or respect, but she has vivid memories of a particular experience as a four-year-old when she felt shame about her body being different from other four year-year-old girls. I'll let Tatia share this experience in her own words.

"It was at a ballet class where we were rehearsing for an upcoming recital of Peter Pan. All the four-year-old girls were playing Tinkerbell, a flock of tiny, pink 'tutued' fairies. We were on a raised platform, waiting in line for the male ballet teacher to lift us off and delicately fly us through the air to the other side of the stage. I kept moving towards the back of the line, delaying my turn. I vividly recall dreading the teacher picking me up because I thought he would notice that I was heavier than the other girls.

Eventually, I jumped down from the stage and ran up to my mother. Even at that young age, I knew admitting that I was embarrassed about my weight was something to be ashamed of. I lied and told her I was scared the teacher would drop me. She told me to stop being so silly and go back on stage. Up I went, only to keep sneaking back in the line. I could feel my Mum's rising frustration, without even making eye contact. I tried a couple of times to run back up and tell her I was scared, only to be dismissed back to the stage with increasing annoyance. Eventually, she'd had enough. I was running up the aisle, in tears as everyone had noticed my behaviour. The other ballerinas were whispering about me, and I could see Mums all around the theatre watching me, confused. My Mum was already packing up her things and storming out of the theatre."

After a series of admonishments, the final comments from her mother really rubbed salt into Tatia's already tender wounds. Finally, she said that she'd never take her back to ballet, adding, "it's no great loss to the ballet scene. You weren't exactly graceful anyway."

Thus began a lifetime of self-loathing that threatened to sabotage her life. As a teenager, she realised that she was never going to meet our society's standard of beauty and so decided that she would make up for that by becoming the person who was the fun one in any group – the outrageous one who made everyone laugh. She reflected that comedy was used as armour and a weapon in her home where, despite the mutual love, affection was not shown verbally or physically. In my experience, others don't tend to realise that the fun person is often covering up a huge amount of pain and heartache. I really understand from my own experience that our lack of self-worth causes us to behave in self-defeating ways in our longing for love and acceptance.

In her desperate search for connection and love, Tatia would have one-night stands with men who didn't care about her at all, hoping she would wake up in the morning to hear declarations of love that never eventuated. Her family would make comments and joke about her perceived behaviour which only exacerbated her deteriorating self-worth. Often comments that are said in jest can be hurtful and in Tatia's case, they were not easily forgotten.

The battle with her body escalated into her early twenties and persistent dieting that always failed became a way of life. Tatia commented, "People assume that if you are sexually assertive, you must be comfortable with your body." This wasn't the case with her, and she found that the more she hated her body, the more she tended to seek approval in loveless intimacy. She described it as a nasty cycle of feeling shame for being overweight, therefore acting in a promiscuous fashion to gain attention from a man to try and feel better about her appearance. This only added to her self-loathing as the men would inevitably lose interest in her.

In her late twenties, she found herself pregnant and hated her body even more as she compared her growing body unfavourably with the glamourous pictures of pregnant women in magazines. She felt that her worthless body had betrayed her again. She wasn't in a serious relationship with her daughter's father, Mick, but they maintained a friendship. However, by the time her daughter was eighteen months old, they had fallen in love. It took many years for her to believe in Mick's love. Her self-loathing made her believe that he was only with her because of their shared child. She knew he didn't find her physically appealing and she put him through so much torture because of her low self-esteem. She did lose weight when they first fell in love but gained weight with the next pregnancy and never lost it again. She wondered if she unconsciously put on weight to see whether Mick would stick around when she was even less attractive. She now reflects that over the almost twenty years they have been together her weight has fluctuated by over forty kilos, yet he remains by her side.

As Tatia entered her forties, she knew that something had to change. She had been dieting for almost thirty years, and her body felt exhausted. I loved the next part of her story when she began to take charge. For her forty-first birthday, she decided to go on a yoga retreat by herself. She wanted to be alone to work out how she could face the next forty years with a better mindset. This is how Tatia described what happened:

"I had a session where I felt a soft white light overwhelm me. I was laying on the floor in Savasana pose, with tears trickling out of my closed eyes. A thought went through my mind that my life would have been so much easier if I'd just loved my body. So many of the mistakes I'd made and trials I'd faced, would have been erased if I'd respected my body and felt worthy. At that moment something in my brain switched. I knew I couldn't face whatever years I had left, struggling with the same shitty self-esteem. I had to accept that I would never look like a supermodel, so I had to find beauty and appreciation for myself in different ways. I returned from that trip with a new ambition to work on improving my confidence. I started therapy with a counsellor to understand why my inner dialogue was so negative."

There was more progress which included marriage counselling with her husband, enabling them to communicate more effectively. This was followed by Tatia exploring the Body Positivity Movement led by Taryn Buffet. Taryn is an internationally recognised keynote speaker and author. On Taryn's website, she states: "It may be hard to imagine, when you see my colourful posts on social media, that the woman who now confidently splashes about at the beach in her bathers used to hate her body so much she was too ashamed to leave the house. And it may be hard to imagine, if this is your current predicament, that you could ever feel the way that I do about my body now. But I'm living proof that it's possible to love the skin you're in wholeheartedly, and in my book Embrace You, I take you through *the very same steps I used to learn to love my own.*" Her mantra on her website reads: "*My body is not an ornament. It is the vehicle to my dreams.*"

Following her viewing of Taryn's documentary *Embrace You*, Tatia joined the movement as a Global Ambassador. You can find more details in the reference section of this book. She was deeply affected by these words, "*My body isn't an ornament, it is a vehicle.*" She has written a brilliant blog about this experience well worth the read. They can be found on her Facebook page,

Tatia worked hard to change her way of thinking, even getting her first tattoo on her forearm of an Enso circle which represents finding beauty in imperfection. Changing her language has been of paramount importance. Rather than saying,

"*My thighs are fat, I need to lose weight*", she began to say things like:

"*I want strong legs to carry me around for all the incredible experiences I want to have.*" I have enjoyed reading Tatia's blogs about her journey and the film clips of her recent adventure with the Body Image Movement.

As her self-image began to change, she was shocked to find herself in a different kind of grief. She became deeply sad for all of the years she had wasted at war with her body.

"*It was a weird time for me as I felt a sense of relief to let the body shaming go. But I felt a new sense of shame for holding on to it for so long. After several months of grieving, I came to my senses and realised that I was simply wasting more time. I accepted that I can't change the past, but I can change how I view it.*" Tatia now uses what she has called her 'wasted energy', working actively in the *Body Image Movement*, running programs that assist other women to find peace with their bodies. I have also mentioned her well-written blogs and look forward to the book she is writing. Her transparency and courage will inspire so many women.

In concluding, I must use Tatia's own words:

"*I have met so many women who are struggling with the same demons I had, for varying reasons. The media with its hyper-sexualisation of women and narrow ideal of beauty, play a big part in this body hating epidemic. The medical industry also has a role in promoting a very limited view of what constitutes healthy. We need to revolutionise how we view our bodies and how we define health. I am passionate about helping people overcome the self-loathing and preventing young people from developing it.*"

14. TATIA'S HEALING TOOLBOX

- Get professional help. Think of it as a tune-up on yourself. Speak to a trained therapist, counsellor, psychologist and get any underlying issues off your chest. I don't think I'd be as mentally healthy today if I hadn't committed to therapy first.

- Curate your social media. Stop following people, friends or celebrities that make you feel bad about yourself. Comparison is the thief of joy. If a post on your social media feed makes you compare your body or looks in any way, delete it, block it, unfollow it! My social media is filled with people and posts that make me laugh, educate or inspire me.

- Change your vocabulary. Swap statements such as, *'I feel fat'* to *'I want to feel comfortable in my body.'* Change *'I hate my fat thighs'* to *'My legs are strong and have to take me on fantastic journeys.'*

- Exercise because you love your body, not to punish it! Find an activity that makes you feel good when you do it. I love to do boxing, dancing, yoga, stretching, hiking, bingeing Netflix. It's all about balance.

- Stop putting moral values on food. There is no good or bad. It's just food, and it gives your body energy. It can also be a wonderful social activity and a way to explore different cultures. Instead of *'I can't eat that – I'll get too fat'* think *'Is that food going to feed my soul and make me happy?'*

- When you are feeling negative about your body, ask yourself *'Who profits from this feeling?'* Take a good look at ads targeting women and see if the message makes you feel inadequate or disrespected. Companies need to make you feel poorly so they can convince you to buy their product. Enough! Don't let them do it anymore!

- Make a pact with close friends that you will no longer allow negative talk about yourselves. We are so used to putting ourselves down to be modest, that we don't realise the deep impact it can have on our psyche. I love hearing people flaunt their talents and great qualities. Don't shy away from it, own it.

- Make time to care for yourself. This one is vital for every aspect of your life. You deserve self-care. I have a mantra I try to say

regularly – 'I understand myself better every day. I am worth celebrating myself. Self-care is a priority. I am worthy of having fun every single day. I take good care of my body and soul. Only I can live out my purpose and choose how I spend my days. I choose to pursue a life that feels good to me. I trust myself. I love myself. I am enough right now.'

CHAPTER 15

Resilience

There are many stories about people who have been knocked down and have managed to get up again. One of the positive aspects of social media is that we get to hear about many uplifting stories that we may never get to experience in other contexts. Sadly, there are also many who cave under the pressure of grief. It is certainly tempting to try and escape pain by using substances or other unhealthy means of avoidance. We have found that there is no easy way out of pain. Usually, with all kinds of grief, there has to be some action taken on our part to find our way through. All of the examples that I am sharing have all made such an effort to make things as right as possible. Even the young people I have written about, once they were given some encouragement, they went into overdrive to become their best selves.

Once Terry found he really could read, he kept reading everything he could lay his hands on and became a successful scholar. Jim found that he wasn't dumb after all and began taking more interest in everything he was asked to do. He really applied himself and decided that he wanted a career as a panel beater. He really deserved his award of apprentice of the year. Joel moved past his feelings of hopelessness and is now holding down two jobs as well as completing his degree in economics. When Jeffrey achieved such success with his win in the robotic competition, he accepted his diagnosis of being dyslexic and decided to work around it and successfully completed an accreditation in electrical engineering.

Maybe because it has been such a significant journey for him, his clients relate that they can always count on him. He has achieved so much against all the odds.

My experience with Martha was an eye-opener. It made me understand how fragile brilliant people can be. I remember a fellow author saying to me once that creative people often pay a price by not always being understood. They are almost always super sensitive. Being isolated on a property certainly made it more difficult for Martha. It took time for her to accept that being different from others did not make her worse or better. She began to enjoy the way her brain worked and how she could express herself. The more people with Martha's skills we have in this world, the better.

I am constantly disturbed by the lack of understanding around the original settlers of our country. They have so much to teach us. I found that when the students I worked with were given the freedom to learn and grow in their own way, they shone. It occurred to me to record some of the bouncing rhythms they used when playing and making their chants into books that they illustrated. This taught me as much as I taught them. I had a group of young students write their own musical using Yothu Yindi's song 'Treaty' as a base. These were a group of ten-year-olds and what they came up with was inciteful and incredibly moving. I wish I still had a copy of what they performed for the school. There are certainly some benefits to today's technology. I hope I live to see the day when we can all live in harmony and respect each other.

Kerri is on fire and is an inspiration for so many people. She certainly walks her talk and is mindful of the shadow that follows her at times. She is determined to keep moving forward and is going from strength to strength. She has just returned from a conference in America and continues as an ambassador, still kicking goals.

Body image is an important topic for most people. There are so many industries making large amounts of money in making women feel bad about their bodies with some very negative consequences. Tatia is doing a great job in sharing her experience and working with women to help them to gain positive self-images and to embrace the notion that "My body isn't an ornament, it is a vehicle."

As mentioned more than once previously, there are so many kinds of grief. Besides losing someone in death, there are other losses that can cause us to grieve. I'd like to introduce you to a few other people who have suffered different kinds of grief and have risen to find their fabulous again… and again… and again.

CHAPTER 16

Polio Did Not Define Her

Picture a bright-eyed, blonde curly haired little girl, full of life and ready to take on the world. Suzette was born with a mild form of spina bifida, causing scoliosis, a significant sideways curve of her spine. She was also born with an indomitable spirit which helped her through her rocky path to adulthood.

Suzette feels that she has buried a great deal of the early memories, but she does remember falling out of a bus and hurting her head at the age of five. Around this time, she became very ill and was diagnosed with Poliomyelitis (or polio) an infection caused by polioviruses. This virus can affect the cells of the central nervous system causing paralysis and Suzette spent the following eighteen months in an iron lung. The iron lung provided breathing support for her paralytic polio. (More information in the reference section at the end of this book)

I can't imagine what it would have been like for this little girl to be encased in this piece of equipment, not being able to breathe without it and not being able to play. At that time there was a polio epidemic and at its peak, there were rows of iron lungs filling hospital wards. Some children only needed to be encased for several weeks, but Suzette was forced to live like this for eighteen months. She spent another two years in the hospital for treatment which included being near the ventilator when she needed it. She has memories of kind relatives who visited her but absolutely no memories of visits from her parents. Suzette was one of eight children, but it is still hard to imagine parents not visiting their sick child in almost five years.

Following her recovery, she retained a significant limp and weakness on the right side of her body. She was often referred to as 'the cripple', and Suzette always felt that her mother, who made a habit of using the term, was ashamed of her. If this wasn't disturbing enough, upon her return home, she suffered inappropriate sexual touching from a member of the family she should have been able to trust. This was something she endured for a number of years. In those days, nobody wanted to know about such things, which must have increased her feelings of isolation.

Despite her tragic early childhood, Suzette grew into a beautiful young woman and was wooed by a handsome young Frenchman. They were both highly intelligent, and at last she had someone who believed in her and with whom she could share stimulating conversations. The added bonus was that she could, at last, be free of her home environment. Against all the odds and with a great deal of courage, Suzette managed to birth two special sons who have given her much joy.

But she still had many challenges to face. It was not commonly known that polio could re-occur in a non-infectious form. This is called post-polio syndrome and Suzette was one of the unlucky ones. She began to experience more and more weakness on her right side and extreme bouts of pain. Each year she felt a more serious decline in movement. She had to give up driving which was a significant loss as she had been very active on the farm she shared with her husband. She could be seen whizzing around on her quad bike always helping with chores on the farm.

When they were in their early sixties, they decided it was time to fulfil their dream of travelling around Australia. It was while they were in Darwin, a pain in her husband's elbow began to get worse. It became so acute he thought he would have it checked out. They were shocked when tests revealed that his pain was the result of bone cancer, so their trip had to be aborted. The arm was removed in an effort to stave off the cancer but it was already too late and Suzette then had the task of nursing him for the next ten months before he passed away.

I met Suzette in 2014 when she was living in a retirement village full of old people with dementia. This was no place for a bright, intelligent woman, who by this time was terrorising people on her mobility scooter. Never one to just sit around, she had a prolific vegetable garden and became involved in activities in the village, but I observed that this place was a real example of God's *waiting room*, and not a place suitable for her. By this time there was very little movement on her right side. Her hand was all but useless and she was getting around with difficulty.

I was very relieved when she was able to sell her unit and assist her son and partner to buy a home which had a very comfortable granny flat for her to live in. She was still very involved in making an exquisite garden and doing her bit around the house, including cooking. Then another calamity beset her. She fell and broke her ankle badly which necessitated it being pinned and a lengthy hospital stay. Just to complicate things more, the foot became infected and resisted efforts to heal with normal antibiotics. She was then given some dangerously strong antibiotics which resulted in her becoming very ill.

She is still suffering the after-effects of the terrible drug. Vertigo and nausea have made it difficult for her to keep her sunny disposition. However she always manages to bounce back. She was told that she would never walk again, but no one tells Suzette that she can't do anything. She will pull herself up as straight as is possible for her, and the look she gives will shrivel any doubts one may have about her capabilities. Unfortunately, she did have another fall and more hospital visits. In the past few years, she has spent more time in the hospital than she has at home. We hope that this time she is home to stay, but we also know she is vulnerable.

With all of the tragic experiences she has suffered, there could be many things that she could grieve about, but she recently told me her strongest grief remains that she wants to do so much more and sometimes feels she is malingering. Of course, nobody who knows her feels this at all. She is always cheerful and shares her laughter and wisdom with many people.

She has a flair with languages and has begun Spanish classes which she is enjoying. Beyond all expectations, she managed to go on a cruise with a friend a few months ago and hopes to fly to visit me this year.

16. SUZETTE'S HEALING TOOLBOX

- Life is precious so make the most of each moment.
- It is always painful to lose your mate, but family is precious and the memories are rich.
- Make a montage of photos from happy times and hang it on your wall to remind you of all of the good times.
- Making a garden and watching things grow is incredibly healing.
- Get rid of any negative people that might inhabit your life.
- The world is full of so many interesting things which keep your brain alive.
- Keeping up with current events helps to stimulate the brain.
- The library is full of treasures.
- Art galleries are wheelchair friendly.
- Social media keeps you in touch with friends all over the world.
- Mobile scooters are the best invention.
- Where there's a will, there's a way. Remember to say, "I can" rather than "I can't".

CHAPTER 17

The Philosophy of Theodosios Albert George Gard

S uch an illustrious name deserves a special mention, but for the remainder of this piece, we might just refer to him as Theo.

Theo was born in rural mid-Devon, England, in a thatched roofed cottage which was part of a group called Trixie's Cottages. He was born an identical twin. His brother George preceded him out of the womb but sadly did not survive. His parents never spoke about George, and although Theo always felt there was something or someone missing, he didn't find out about his brother for a number of years. He had no idea what caused his brother's death, but he had been aware of being in a continual state of grief his whole life for a brother he had never known.

Recently I saw adult identical twins interviewed and they viewed themselves as sharing one complete brain. They joked about it, but when questioned, they explained that one was extremely left-brained – practical, analytical and methodical in his thinking, while the other was more creative and artistic. The left/right brain theory has been rather debunked. However, we do see examples that make us wonder. I have always seen myself predominantly right-brained, but when I started running my own business, I was forced to develop more analytical skills.

If there is any truth in the theory, it would be interesting to speculate how it might have been for Theo who, if we were to follow the theory, would certainly fit into the right brained category, being very creative and extremely caring. Dr Christian Jarette (Brain Myths) wrote that:

"There is more than a grain of truth to the left-brain, right-brain myth. While they look alike, the two hemispheres of the brain do function differently. For example, it's become almost common knowledge that in most people the left brain is dominant for language. The right hemisphere, on the other hand, is implicated more strongly in emotional processing and representing the mental states of others. However, the distinctions aren't as clear cut as the myth makes out - for instance, the right hemisphere is involved in processing some aspects of language, such as intonation and emphasis."

We can of course only speculate what effect losing his identical twin had on Theo's long term decision making or lifestyle choices, but suffice to say that he often felt incomplete and there was grief around that fact.

Many years later as Theo approached his seventieth year, his friend Carol Curtis mentioned to him that she believed that this early grief was at the root of some of the difficulties that he had faced in his life. She suggested that a cranial-sacral session might reveal something that could help him find closure. As it was her practice, she offered to conduct this for him.

Cranio-Sacral Therapy is performed on a fully-clothed person. Using a very soft touch, Carol was able to monitor the rhythm of Theo's craniosacral system to detect potential restrictions and imbalances. In order to release these blockages, she gently manipulated the membranes that surround the brain and spinal cord.

The craniosacral system is made up of the membranes and fluid that surround, protect and nourish the brain and spinal cord. It extends from the bones of the head, face and mouth to the sacrum or tailbone area. As this system directly impacts the central nervous system, he was given the opportunity to release any patterns or blockages that were restricting his ability to move past trauma.

Theo approached the session with some scepticism but was willing for this much-trusted friend to take him to a place he had never been before. He is still slightly bemused by the session and has attempted to apply logic to make sense of his experience. However, it was an experience that he cannot deny.

It wasn't long into the session before he envisioned finding himself in a womb filled with warm fluid, and felt himself fighting to get out. He kept coming up against a barrier that stopped him from moving forward. There was a sensation of panic as he felt himself bouncing up against rubbery walls. Eventually, he found that he could punch his way out, but the whole birthing process took a great deal of effort. He felt exhausted and experienced an overwhelming sense of grief.

Following the session, Theo became very emotional, and in one of the rare moments in his life, he found tears falling. With encouragement from Carol, he allowed himself to let the copious tears flow for around ten minutes. It had been a profound experience.

As a child, Theo grew to be a rather gentle soul, and as a young married man, he was accused of possessing no 'street-cred' by his wife. She was insinuating that he was a bit of a pushover and not someone worthy of admiration from fashionable young people. Whilst he had gained much wisdom in his later years, his inability to hold a grudge is still present and the word hate is never present in his vocabulary.

Theo always showed a strong empathy for people and was always unconsciously a deep thinker. In the 1970s, he launched into some self-development work which was very in vogue at that time. He initially followed the work of Carlos Castaneda. However, as time went on, he withdrew from the self-help movement, vowing to use his own resources to regulate his life. Maybe his creative spirit did not want to be tethered, and he preferred to adopt an almost *non-thinking* stance which better suited his personality. However, he still demonstrates a strong philosophical streak and often comes up with deep, almost meditative pieces of wisdom. One of his recent posts reflected some of the strategies he has used to keep his spirits up when he is tempted to fade back into grief.

"Often I post my paintings about the turmoils I/we often face in our lives...but tonight, its all about those times we choose to forget them and look towards a future of cruising through! A better one for us, the happier life we want to have! So dream on the ocean waves, gentle ones. My abstracts are

*all about how I feel about me, the world we live in, how that impacts on our
lives. So, I often portray that in spidery images...the intricate webs we lead in
our life's journey because of personal issues and what affects us outside our
personal world...but we can summon up our personal strengths to how we
feel about us, our world and how we deal with it! We just have to be strong!"*

Authenticity was always extremely important to him, and he
pondered the reason his three marriages ultimately failed. It appeared
that he attracted women who were needy and initially drawn to his
warmth and gentleness, but then wanted to dominate him. He even
used the term *gaslighting* to describe the behaviour he witnessed from his
wives. Maybe they misread his gentleness for weakness. If so, they were
wrong. Theo has always been very much his own person. His creative
disposition meant he preferred not to do much planning but rather take
each day as it came. This was not an unusual stance adopted by many
artists.

As is often the way with caring people, he found himself quite gifted
at being able to assist others to find solutions and enhance self-esteem,
whilst perhaps neglecting to do the same for himself. On a recent trip to
England, he found himself in a vulnerable moment, breaking down in
front of his sister when he witnessed her interaction with her children
and grandchild. The realisation that he would never experience this
interaction with his own flesh and blood overwhelmed him at that
moment. It was confirmed in his third marriage that it was highly
probable that there could be no children.

Animals were always a priority for him, and when I met him,
his family included two very senior Shih Tzu dogs called Harry and
Pippa. They were the loves of his life and totally devoted to him. It
was heartbreaking to watch how their devotion caused them to hang
onto life longer than their health dictated. Inevitably the time came
when Theo knew that he could no longer allow Harry to suffer and
the dreaded trip to the vet became a reality. Two years later this post
appeared on Theo's Facebook page:

*"I took Pippa today to the vet for her rainbow trip. She was nearly 17
years of age but kinda told me over the last 24 hrs (stayed up with her the*

last 2 nights), that she was ready to join her brother Harry in doggie heaven. Have shed tears but happy that she's now free of pain and suffering. Our pets to some of us are really special. For me, my two little ones helped me through some pretty hard parts of my life. They gave me unconditional love and caring. They were always there for me, no matter what, with a wag! So, now my two very special friends are united. Will always think of them and thank them for being a special part of my life...Thank you, Harry and Pippa."

I don't think I would have been the only one to be moved to tears after having read this post. Harry and Pippa had been Theo's family, so his grief was understandable. We cannot underestimate the grief felt at the loss of a much-loved pet. This was the main reason that I felt moved to write this piece. I have always thought that many people do not understand the huge grief that lovers of their pets experience when they leave us. Research has shown that grieving the death of our animals can be just as painful as grieving for a family member or friend. When we lose a family member, we usually receive understanding and sympathy, but when people, who have never had an animal that was part of the family, see their friend who has lost a beloved pet, in deep mourning, they often feel it is an overreaction – after all 'it is just a dog'. So there are no public rituals where there can be closure, it is often just the lonely trip to the vet. Maybe if we could all realise how intense and beautiful the bond is between people and their animals, their grief would be more understood. There needs to be acknowledgement so that the animal owner can integrate the death into the next step of their lives and be able to move forward. Theo lives by himself in a dear little cottage and when both of his beloved pets had gone, they left a huge hole in his life.

Theo had explained that when his last marriage ended with his wife moving away a number of years ago, she planned to take one of the dogs, but he insisted that Harry and Pippa stay together. They were very much a team and, in a marriage where he was often alone, he had been the one to look after them. They were indeed his family and were totally reliant on him. People would enjoy seeing their happy faces as they travelled around with their master wherever he went. They were always there for him, providing companionship and loyalty when it sometimes felt the world had let him down.

Harry was the first to go and the loss was real. Pippa was becoming frail and needed extra care which Theo lovingly provided, knowing the day was not far away when he would have to say goodbye to this little friend who had filled such a hole in his, sometimes, lonely life. He had tried to prepare himself for the time when he would have to let her go, but it is never possible to do that. He would look around for her, almost expecting her to appear around the corner – then the realisation that he was never going to see her sweet face or her happy wagging tail, would sweep over him. He would never again feel her cuddled up to him on the couch – their breathing often in sync. Even writing this brings tears to my eyes and I wish that I could have joined with him in some kind of wake. I have learnt that some kind of closure can be an important step.

A few years ago, Theo allowed me to read an autobiographical account of his father's life. It told of an earnest Christian man who had devoted his life to the service of others as a missionary. He had led an extraordinary life and had met Theo's mother, a lovely Cretan lady, in 1946 in Athens during the Greek civil war. His mother came back with his father to England where they were married. Two years later, Theo and his twin were born.

Theo had grown up in the era in which parents had the mistaken belief that fathers don't show affection to boys. His mother lavished him with many demonstrations of her love, but even though his father was always kind, he refrained from too many physical demonstrations. Theo watched his sister enjoying lots of hugs and cuddles from his father. As he watched from the sidelines, he yearned to be on the receiving end of some of those demonstrations of affection, but they never came. He often wondered if his father loved him or why he couldn't articulate that he loved him. A particularly moving revelation came to Theo when he discovered that his father had chosen a special title for an autobiography he'd written in the 1980s called, *Letters to Theo*. This was his declaration of love that was a beautiful reminder of the father he had admired and loved for so many years.

Theo had a resurgence of his creativity during his retirement years where he has rediscovered his love of painting. He uses all kinds of materials, sharing his creations on Facebook. His various works are inspired by Picasso. There is the corrugated iron masterpieces, repurposed canvases, muted colours and beautifully vibrant, rather joyous pieces. His mood can almost be measured by what he produces in his beautifully messy painting room. A framed picture of his namesake, St Theodosius looks over him in his art space. Usually, he has no idea about what he is going to paint but is easily inspired with the help of a little liquid refreshment.

In Theo's case, he found his fabulous under the guise of new creativity that he accomplishes in his unrestricted painting attire that simply consists of a pair of underpants as he too becomes a human canvas. His painting has been a help to him as he has come to terms with the loss of his life as a family man and two little dogs that gave him unconditional love. So often when we are getting our lives together following grief, our bodies can respond in ways that are often difficult to navigate. We understand that we suffer emotionally, but I also believe that there are often physical effects. Theo's spine problems escalated and he began suffering debilitating, excessive pain which greatly restricted his mobility. He is now receiving ongoing treatment and there has been a vast improvement in his mobility which of course is lifting his mood. He has been very courageous through this process and now he is able to get around more and not so stuck in time, waiting for little footsteps or gentle love licks.

Theo and I spent several hours on the phone discussing what I would write in this piece. These kinds of conversations always bring up memories and can be quite painful. I am always aware of this and try to be sensitive. Following our long conversation, Theo found himself going straight to his studio, where he produced a painting that expressed all of what he was feeling. 'The rainbow through the cobwebs' just happened and when I saw it, I felt that his rainbow is beginning to shine through the cobwebs and that his life is transitioning into a positive place. It is such an appropriate illustration for the cover of this book.

Now that his back is healing, Theo is looking at what he can do in his community to help others. He has many gifts and has so much to offer in a healing space. Meanwhile, his paintings have taken on a life of their own. He doesn't know where his inspiration is coming from but there has been a shift of some kind and it is exciting. I hope he will have an exhibition at some point, but at this point, he is content to let it all flow. He posted his thoughts in another blog:

"My abstract art is so much about feelings, my stuff. I don't strive to get into the art world to sell or even get into the thing of having an exhibition, but to express my life through art works and help others through maybe a few words of explanation. If through my stuff I can help another person get through their stuff, I'm a happy man!"

I am still hoping he will change his mind about an exhibition and I am proud to have that special painting on my cover which followed our conversation. It says so much and is a reminder that the cobwebs can disappear as we recognise our rainbow.

Theo recently posted a quote that I felt quite pertinent. It is from Psychic Medium Nikki:

> "One of the most courageous decisions you'll ever make is to finally let go of what is hurting your heart and soul."

17. THEO'S HEALING TOOLBOX

- Be careful not to wallow in grief. Certainly, face it and accept it then try to find an avenue to fill up the spaces in between the grieving.

- There are all sorts of activities – you may not feel like doing anything but have a go. Painting happens to be something I find very healing.

- I make a point of looking out of my window each morning and taking in everything I can see, it could be a bird making a nest, the different colours of flowers and leaves, a lizard running amongst the grass. I savour every little piece of nature. Recently I have begun to marvel at the tiny little flowers that push their way through the matted grass and reveal their pretty little petals. Nature is amazing.

- Observe the stuff we go through in our lives, the maelstroms some of us have experienced, yet finally, when we see the colour, we can get through joy and happiness that can come our way when we listen to our heart.

- Yesterday was yesterday, tomorrow is another day, but today is your day, whatever it might bring.

- My mantra: All you need is love. We all do...from family, friends, partners, lovers, pets, acquaintances, strangers...but also to give that love out, with a bit of compassion and understanding mixed in... spread it! Your world and yours in it will surely become a better place

CHAPTER 18

Transforming a Forgotten Village

The story about the miracles Donna Cooper is managing to achieve in Cambodia deserves a special mention. I had begun to write her biography, but sadly there were factors that prevented me from completing it. Donna, however, has given me permission to share some of her story.

Donna does not have many happy memories of her childhood. When I think of my children at six years old, I can't imagine that they could have been able to serve in a shop by themselves, but from the age of six, Donna was expected to do chores well beyond her years including being left in charge of the family shop and selling newspapers at the local Royal Australian Airforce Base. She had no choice but to develop an amazing resilience which has carried her through circumstances where her safety has been threatened.

School was difficult for her for all sorts of reasons, and she was not encouraged to pursue an education, so at the age of fourteen, she left school. She took the chance to escape the nightmare of her home and ventured into the wide world where she soon began to see the benefits of an education. This valuable lesson made her determined to ensure her children received the best education she could give them.

Fortunately, she met a young man who saw something special in her. They fell in love and eventually married. He tried to understand what her life had been like and was always supportive. Three children were born and Donna was determined that they would have all of the benefits that she missed out on. It always amazes me that there are some born into a less than supportive homes and go on to repeat the pattern with their own children. Then there are others like Donna, who determine that they will break the pattern and provide stability for their family.

Donna had a vision to give as many girls as possible the opportunities she missed out on. However, without any funds of her own, she faced the challenge of how to acquire enough funds to furnish her vision. There were times that everything seemed against her and there were even those who took advantage of her generous nature, but every time she felt like giving up, she focused on what needed to be done and managed to find a way.

She began by collecting every piece of clothing that was not being worn by her children. The discarded clothes were of very good quality, and following a gentle wash, a good press and an infusion of love, they looked as good as new. She had been selling since she was six years old and this early sales experience stood her in great stead. She sold every piece of clothing for almost what it had originally been worth. Initial success set off a chain reaction of trawling through second-hand shops for designer clothes or at the very least, clothes of good quality. She was able to sell them for a good mark-up price.

The logical upgrade was to have a store full of pre-loved clothing. Following a few false starts, she was given the opportunity to take over the lease from a couple who were moving on from a little shop in the main street of Woodend, Victoria. There was no spare money for a fit-out, but with their creativity, expeditions to the tip provided bits and pieces, and she and her husband were able to fit out a unique little store with discarded timber and other materials that gave it a rather bohemian, rustic look. Bohemian fits Donna as she is an incredibly free spirit. She reminds me of a pixie with her lovely face and long dreadlocks. Her lithe body is always on the move. Stillness is not something that comes easily to Donna. Her brain is always busy, full of new ideas and she has managed to work marvels with very little budget.

The store in Woodend was an instant success, and soon Donna was able to move on from the onerous task of refurbishing second-hand clothes and look towards buying new stock. Three trips to Bali produced colourful alternate clothing and native curios, which also sold very well. Her hard work enabled her to send her children to college. They have all completed a tertiary qualification and her younger son is studying medicine. When Donna says she is going to achieve something, you had better believe it. The evidence of her ability to role model shines out in her daughter, Sam, who in turn has taken up the gauntlet for women.

Donna's business progressed, enabling her to open her beautiful store in Daylesford, Victoria where she employed other young women who were able to learn so much from her. Not only did they learn how to run a business, but Donna also taught them incredible life skills, including integrity, caring about others and how to live in a world that is sometimes hard to understand. Donna became well known for supporting the women in the community and encouraging them to become self-sufficient. Her dedication to her vision and selfless determination changed the lives of hundreds of women and their families.

Donna then became aware of the acute suffering of the people in Cambodia and after much travail, she and her family decided to assist one of the poorest villages in the province of Kampong Thom. There had been no sanitation in the village when she first visited and children were suffering from scabies and head lice. She learnt how to build water wells that would provide the village with fresh water. The village now has proper wells, vegetable gardens and the houses are kept neat and tidy. Most importantly, it has a beautiful school where children are gaining a good education that will allow them to gain meaningful employment formerly denied them. At the school, you will find students in the media room learning skills such as coding and other sophisticated programs that will assist them to find jobs in the future. In the library, which is filled with many up to date books, children are seen lying on bean bags reading. The classrooms are well furnished and students have a curriculum that will serve them for when they leave this place and look for work. While mostly the teachers are native Cambodians, the main language spoken is English. The children have been taught how to make the best of themselves and their big smiles are a testament to how they love their educational adventures. Photos reveal clean, healthy young women and men who have learnt skills that will carry them through for the rest of their lives. Of course, this didn't happen overnight. There are many stories to be told of the heartaches and pitfalls Donna and her family encountered along the way.

As I have mentioned previously, I hope one day a movie is made about this incredible woman and her family. What a powerful role model. Donna and her family managed to transform the village through her vision. She believes women can do anything they set their minds to. By her example, both young men and women have come to believe in themselves. She is continuing to promote sustainable change one village at a time in Cambodia. She also provides opportunities for local students in Australia to attend *MishCam* once a year where they become embroiled in the day to day activities of the village and its school. They come away feeling they have had a lifetime of experiences which will forever inspire them to keep this chain of positive role modelling going forever.

One of her latest projects has been to open a spa in Phnom Penn where young women are given the opportunity to learn business and beauty skills. With her daughter Sam, she has created *The Sew Good Company*, in which women in the village are given the opportunity to make lovely clothes that are sold to 55 outlets in Australia. *The Sew Good Company* provides their employees with paid maternity leave, sick leave, free health care, free education and training. These kinds of work conditions are rare in many places in Cambodia. It is heartening to see that this innovative company is being recognised and has been featured in some highly respected fashion magazines. A well-deserved reward for so much hard work.

As the director of The Cambodian Kids Foundation, Donna has had to orchestrate fundraising activities which go towards the school she has built. She has managed to build a loyal team who support the phenomenal work she continues to do. It is almost incomprehensible to understand that this woman, along with her family, not only had this incredible vision, she continues to do everything she can to make it happen. Her example inspires her own children to want to provide sustainable systems that can be carried through for future generations, whilst saving precious lives. She continues to make many sacrifices.

I have only given a few glimpses of what Donna and her family have managed to achieve. What I haven't been able to tell you about are some of the horrific experiences and the times when Donna wondered how she could keep going, but she did.

There have been many moments of grief. Times when it seemed that her dream was impossible, but every time she gets knocked down, she finds a way to get up again and keep going. What a powerful example of finding her fabulous again, …again…and again.

18. DONNA'S HEALING TOOLBOX

- When you believe in something, never give up.
- Be clear about your vision.
- Scope up what you see needs to be done.
- Don't be afraid to take risks and think outside the square.
- Brainstorm every possibility of raising money.
- Look for resources – don't be afraid to ask, there are people out there who do want to help.
- Don't let anybody put you off your game.
- Help women know that they can do anything.
- There is always a way.
- When you feel like giving up, look for another way or seek advice.
- Love, love, love!

CHAPTER 19

The Power of the Dreamtime

Shirley Cross has inspired many with her quiet determination and incredible courage in fighting for the best outcomes for her family under often difficult conditions. Shirley has a different story. One that she has had to learn to unravel but which makes so much sense to her now.

Brought up in a farming community, Shirley now recognises that she was unworldly, with no idea about the harshness of what was happening in the real world. As a child, she was drawn to her father and loved hearing his stories and his simple way of explaining the world. His words always made so much sense to her, but his views on life seemed to be at odds with her mother's thinking.

As a young child, she was often puzzled by the reactions of others to her family. There was something she couldn't put her finger on. At the school bus stop, she encountered a man who seemed to focus on her as he ranted about his support for the White Australia Policy. She didn't understand what he was talking about and had no idea his remarks were directed at her or her family.

Her father instilled in her a philosophy about death which seemed very practical. His belief around death and grieving sounded so simplistic yet very logical. He would tell her that when a person passes away, they no longer have any earthly feelings, so grieving about the death of someone is just for ourselves. We need to adjust to being without them and deal with our feelings of grief. He was quite matter-of-fact about it and was adamant that when he went, it would be his time and so there would be no need to grieve. He insisted that they must go on with their lives as he had lived his life and that was it. Shirley believes that these early teachings influenced her in the way she deals with her own experiences of grief.

Sadly, her father was ill for much of her growing years, but he always took time to share his stories. These moments are deeply entrenched in her memory. She identified with her father, but there were many times when she felt she didn't belong anywhere. There was so much that she didn't understand. She loved to paint but grew frustrated when she found herself unable to paint the pretty landscapes and flowers that seemed to be the genre of other budding artists. She found herself drawn to entirely different subjects. She was passionate about nature and happily painted lizards, snakes and other inmates of the Australian bush. She would often complete her work by filling the canvas with dots and significant markings. She had no idea why she did this, and when she compared her work to others, she felt ashamed of what she had produced. Years later I am thrilled to see some of this work adorning her walls. They are exquisite pictures that hint of the magic of the Dreamtime.

As a mature young woman, she often felt that she was a black woman in a white woman's body. She could not understand the world of white thinking. She had always had an acute intuition and a certain knowing that seemed to be at odds with many of those around her. She observed people making decisions that she knew would not give them a satisfactory result. How could they not know? Yet often she was made to feel that she was the one that was out of step with the world she lived in. It was very confusing.

Most of her life she had no idea that her father was Aboriginal. Nobody explained it to her. It was later in her life that it all made sense, and that her attitudes about grief sprang from her father's Indigenous heritage and the ways he had learnt to deal with loss. As she looks back on photos, she can recognise the Aboriginal features in her father and also in herself.

I am grateful for the knowledge that I have gained from Aboriginal people. At first, I didn't understand that individuals, who looked more white than black, were so adamant that they identified as Aboriginal. Now I understand that even though they may look predominately white, the Indigenous component of their DNA has proven to be dominant. This causes a great deal of discrimination from both the white and black community. I have mentioned Josephine Cashman who is passionate about her Indigenous heritage. She has devoted her life to doing what she can to assist her people out of victimhood, yet she is often accused of being too white.

When I worked with the Kuku Yalanji people in Mossman, North Queensland, for a number of years, I learnt that they had a spiritual connection, unlike anything I had seen in the white community. I wonder if we once had this connection but filtered it out with the lifestyle we developed. It broke my heart to see the disconnection that happened in a divided community with little understanding for a people whose heritage went back at least 60,000 years.

I learnt that Aboriginal spirituality gives meaning to everything in Aboriginal communities. It affects all aspects of life including relationships with each other. It helps them explain all aspects of the environment they live in and their amazing kinship to the land. This is often expressed through their rituals. I found that even those who escaped into substance abuse still retained a spirituality and knowledge that we have lost. I was always touched when some of my indigenous students, who would sometimes display behaviour that teachers found difficult, would become completely absorbed when participating in dance or song. They could also tell me when someone had died, even though the death had happened far away. I would ask them how they knew and they would shrug their shoulders or make a comment, "The birds told us." It was a consistent pattern. Their intuition is highly developed and I believe we all can fine tune our intuition. I also believe that we are at this time closer to a time when we become more connected to each other and through Josephine, I know that true Aboriginal leaders want to share their knowledge with us. There is a great deal of ignorance that causes racist slurs. Many point their fingers to the Aboriginal drunk in the gutter, or to the examples of rape, theft and domestic violence. It is important for us to recognise that regrettably, we have many examples of this behaviour in our own society. I was shocked when I was explaining some work I was engaged in with a relative, he made a comment, "Oh, do some of them work?" I have had the privilege of working with and getting to know outstanding Aboriginal people who still receive racist slurs and disrespect.

While conversing with Shirley, I was reminded of all of this and have come to realise that missing out on participating in what was her inherent right, and what she instinctively knew, has caused her a great deal of grief. Shirley has had many things to grieve about in her lifetime but in her own words, she has said that her biggest grief has been that she is misunderstood.

Shirley is intensely curious and always looking for answers. This led her to seek spiritual guidance from an early age. The internet became a great source of discovery for her. She was drawn to material by Wayne Dyer around forty years ago and continues to expand her spiritual practices and knowledge. I am often astounded at her wise interpretations of what some of us may find hard to understand.

It has been a special experience to get to know Shirley. Many of us would be forgiven if we supposed her biggest grief was what she is best known for these days – the mother of Perry Cross who is probably the best-known quadriplegic in Australia. I wish I could do justice to her story and hope that one day she will feel free to tell it from her own perspective. I now understand that of course, her experiences of the past twenty-four years have certainly brought much grief, but her deepest grief was feeling that she has never felt the belonging that was part of her birthright. It is only in recent years that she has been able to embrace her own Aboriginality and it has helped her make sense of who she is. The wisdom her father shared with her as a young girl has helped her traverse the last twenty-four years.

In 1994 she received the unforgettable call that turned her world upside down. Her son Perry had been hurt in a football accident, and the news from the hospital did not sound good. His parents were asked to come quickly, and as they travelled from The Gold Coast to Brisbane, Shirley kept thinking about how self-sufficient Perry had always been. He hadn't needed his parents, and the fact that they were now being called urgently to go to his side, made her know intuitively that this was something serious.

The next few days, the situation went from bad to worse. He was originally sent to a hospital which was not equipped to deal with the injuries Perry had sustained. Also, the doctor allocated to the case was unable to give them any answers. It took some reshuffling and time for Perry's father and Shirley to begin to understand what they were going to have to deal with. It was at least four days before they could comprehend the full extent of what was happening. At this stage, Perry could not talk, move, breathe or even roll his eyes around. This wasn't like someone passing from this life, this was a completely new ball game. Trying to maintain the belief, instilled in her by her father, that you can always create some good out of a bad situation, Shirley had to listen and listen to see what the next steps were going to be.

This period of waiting and listening took months, and Shirley never felt that she was given the full picture about what should be happening with Perry's healing process. She made up her mind to stick to her determination to always make the best of a bad situation and be grateful for what they had. Her strong spiritual belief certainly gave her strength at this time, and anyone who knows Shirley can testify to the strength and courage she has shown throughout Perry's journey.

Shirley's spirituality is strongly connected to nature and nature's gifts. Hence she initially baulked at Perry having to use a ventilator to breathe. Having a strong belief that nature would play a big part in Perry's healing, she thought that using a ventilator would interrupt a natural healing process. However, in time she accepted that the ventilator was created by someone in a science laboratory and so this was a gift of human intervention given to Perry to help him breathe. As she watched her beloved son lying there unable to move, she realised that she would have to accept that there was going to be a little more than nature involved in the process to assist him. It became clear to her that nature was involved when humans were given the skills and knowledge to help people have a better life while they are here on this planet. She reflected that animals are here to teach us lessons as are all facets of nature, but as humans, we are here on a higher plain and once we connect to nature, living on the higher plain, then we can create more than the birds do. So now she felt that she had to accept at this time a ventilator was necessary for Perry to breathe. I love the way her mind works.

It was extremely painful watching Perry each day, not knowing what they were watching for; whether a blink of an eye, or any tiny movement. As Shirley and Perry's father stood by his bed, they were dealing with the feeling of helplessness that threatened to engulf them. The predictions were dire, it seemed that everybody just expected him to die. What if he did survive? Would he be in a nursing home for the rest of his life? What a prognosis for this handsome young man, the promising football star, who had always been so healthy. The negativity was overwhelming, and all conversations around Perry's condition and treatment only focused on difficulties.

In time, Perry was able to blink, one blink for yes, two blinks for no. Shirley had always been open and honest with her kids, and so when she could see how people were dealing with what seemed to be an impossible situation, she asked Perry if he wanted to keep going. She would understand that sometimes it is easier just to slip away. He responded by blinking, communicating a strong yes. He did want to go on living, and at that moment, Shirley knew that she was never going to give up on a full recovery. That blink was like a breath of fresh air to her. Here was someone who wanted to live. It didn't make it any easier, in fact, it forced them to find new ways of moving forward.

She devised a way, a kind of game, to help them move forward. They made up a plan for escaping from the hospital 'prison'. With each tiny bit of progress, they would begin 'digging' under the bed, then under the hospital floor, digging tunnels to get out. Even the slightest improvement would get them digging closer to the tunnel exit. This was a way for her to cope and to show Perry how much they were coping with what was going on and the people they were dealing with from all aspects of life – not just the medical team. She knew that mental and emotional issues were threatening to sabotage their ability to manage what was happening.

The digging was progressing slowly, and it was a really tough gig. Shirley would say things like, "Well, we are under the bed, but now we have to dig deeper under the foundations of the hospital, and then we have to dig right along here, so there is a lot of work for us to do."

This goal to get out of prison was the impetus to keep going. Perry was communicating that he wanted to be out of there by Christmas and Shirley would think to herself, "Well, nobody else is thinking that is possible, but since you want to do this, let's do it." So, they kept pushing and pushing to keep things moving. Perry was not about to give up, and Shirley knew it was important that he felt fully supported in knowing there was not going to be any giving up.

Shirley recounts that there was no time for grief at that moment. They were all working together on a project, and they needed to concentrate to ensure that the project was a success. This gave them something to do without being consumed by the grief of it all. Shirley found her ability to block out unpleasant memories was an imperative survival tool at the time. We can subconsciously block out things so successfully that they never come back. She chose not to allow depression to overtake her, but there were times when she cried for hours. This was mainly because she couldn't get people to understand that she had a deeper insight into what kinds of assistance she knew were needed to dig deeper under the hospital to gain freedom. She was simply ignored.

With all of the outward resilience she has shown, Shirley recognises that grief does build up in the body and many years later will force its way out in a rare expression of tears. She recommends the use of meditation and taking time out to clear the energy. Shirley calls it 'living', when we balance all aspects of our lives.

Having worked for a lot of years with people in many contexts, including those with disabilities, I have witnessed that relationships change when there is a significant event and many marriages do not survive. In my own experience following Matt's accident, my marriage hung together for his sake but ultimately disintegrated. Sadly, Shirley's marriage did not survive and she was left with many difficult decisions to make on her own.

Shirley has never given up and has found there is always a way to sort things out. It is a testimony to her dedication that while accompanying Perry to the occupational therapy room and other therapies, she would engross herself in a myriad of books from all over the world, finding out as much as possible about others who had suffered the same spinal injury as Perry. This gave her ammunition when specialists would be totally negative about the prognosis for any kind of recovery for her son.

Shirley and Perry were inspired by the story of Elizabeth Twistington Higgins, a dancer whose career was cut short by polio. Though she was confined to a wheelchair by day and an iron lung by night, she continued her activities as a teacher and director-choreographer of a dance group. She also began to paint with a paintbrush held in her mouth. Since Perry was only able to move his head, Shirley thought he also could use his mouth to become an artist. She collected books and articles hoping to inspire Perry, but he totally rejected the idea. He did not see a future as an artist that painted with his mouth. Feeling a little daunted, she was concerned about the limited options available for someone with Perry's lack of movement. As things have transpired, she needn't have worried.

Shirley recalled that when Perry was at school, barely a day would pass without him getting into trouble for talking too much. Little did she know that his ability to talk would make him a powerful ambassador and that he would find his new life as a motivational speaker. With his words and special smile, he is able to exude tremendous strength and vitality. He has become a well-known identity who inspires many people and is Australia's first motivational speaker on life support. He is also the first Australian quadriplegic to complete a university degree on campus, graduating with a Bachelor of Communications from Bond University and authoring the autobiography *Still Standing*.

The Perry Cross Spinal Research Foundation (PCSRF) came into being very early in Perry's recovery as Shirley and Perry had the desire to find a cure for anyone with any debilitating spinal injuries. With their determination, it has continued to grow in its ability to raise money for groundbreaking research. Perry travels and speaks to groups nationally and globally. Shirley has watched him emerge as a powerful leader who never loses sight of his mantra 'Everything is possible'.

One of his early highlights was to travel to America where he met up with the former Superman star, Christopher Reeve, who sustained the same kind of injury a year after Perry had his accident. Christopher was inspired by the determination and courage shown by Perry and urged him to be the one to find a cure. They remained in touch until Christopher's death.

When Shirley is asked about what she has learnt from her journey so far, she says that she had to learn to stop caring. She remembers her internal dialogue:

I would give my life for his. I would give this. I would give that, and on and on." She believes this was a necessary stage before she entered the excruciating pain of letting go. "You can only do a certain amount of caring before letting the other person go and allowing them to grow their own wings and fly," she stated. She believes that caring can hold people back in quite profound ways and letting them fly is an essential part of healing.

I remember my own experience of having to let go, and I think for a mother, this is one of the most difficult things we have to do. Sometimes this very act can cause an enormous amount of grief. Of course, Shirley is an ever-present figure in the background; always only a phone call away and always willing to drop anything at a moment's notice if Perry needs an extra hand. Her strength and wisdom are rock solid after so many years of battling the system and naysayers and seeing her son break new ground in his desire to live a busy fulfilling life which involves their never-ending search for a cure. This means ensuring that no stone remains unturned in the support for further research and advancement in the treatment, management and cure for paralysis.

There have been many stories written about Perry. There is more information in the reference section. I wanted this piece to be more about Shirley and how her Aboriginal heritage has influenced the way she deals with situations. Whilst she has ongoing grief as she watches her son navigate this world as a C2 quadriplegic, I felt moved when she shared the underlying grief in her life in which she feels that she is often misunderstood.

I believe that when you have a mother like Shirley, who never stops learning and gaining as much knowledge as she can, everything **is** possible. She inspires us all

CHAPTER 20

The Final Word

Just prior to writing this book, my acupuncturist asked me to recall the happiest time of my life. Without a pause, I replied that it was right now. He looked puzzled. Why would someone who had passed through childhood, forged through young adulthood, handled matronhood and now in the autumn years of her life say that this was the best time in her life?

I think there is much that I have written in this book that would explain why I feel this way. For the first time in my life, I have a clear understanding of who I am and what I am here to do. For most of my life, I felt I didn't belong anywhere, which I realise is not an unusual experience for many people. Gratitude is a word that frequently enters my mind these days because I am so grateful for all of the experiences of my life that have led me to where I am now. I mentioned in my year of pain that nothing seemed to be happening for me, but I now know I was just in that space between my being fabulous again …and again.

Sharing the stories of a handful of people has been such a privilege. It is gratifying to learn from each other. I have encouraged each person to share what practices helped them get through their grievous times. There are some common practices that assisted them to keep going. Meditation is a practice commonly used by some, as is actively practising the Law of Attraction which includes changing our language and monitoring our thoughts. These are certainly practices that have assisted me in my search for meaning.

I love the daily practices Kerri has with her family. She is certainly walking her talk and inspiring so many others. Kerri also likes to remind us that there are days when we don't feel so fabulous, and that's okay. We know that tomorrow is another day and it is absolutely worth every effort we make.

In every case, there have been experiences of grief that could have caused a derailment and in some cases did so, but only temporarily. Each person in this book has picked themselves up and moved forward. Of course, I have only been able to write fragments of their stories. Each have their own magical tale to tell, and each have identified their desire to inspire others. At the end of the day, we are all here for each other. We never have to be alone.

We are all on our own journey and there will be cobwebs along the way hindering our progress in our quest to find our fabulous again. It makes all the difference to our outcomes if, even when things get tangled up in cobwebs, we can look for the rainbow that is always there shining through the cobwebs.

After rain there's a rainbow
After a storm there's calm
After the night there's a morning
And after an end
There's a new beginning. **DAYSTAR**

CHAPTER 21

Summing Up – What is Grief?

A s a final word, I would like to leave a summary of the grief process emphasising some points from the healing toolbox and garnered from research and experiences of a number of people I have interviewed.

We have spoken about the belief that grief happens when we experience the loss of someone or something. It can be the loss of a loved one, loss of a pet, a loss of an old way of life, a loss of dignity. There are so many reasons that we can experience grief. It can make us feel really ill, yet it is a normal response to a life event and takes time to adjust. I mentioned in chapter one that we cannot put a time limit on grief, but there are some actions that do help.

I have come to terms with the knowledge that grief is not an illness and cannot be cured, nor can we hurry it along. There is no band-aid big enough to cover it up. I have mentioned ad nauseam that no two people grieve or heal in the same way. It depends a lot on our past experiences, spiritual beliefs, and also our personality. Whilst there is no clear blueprint to dealing with grief, I certainly found it helpful to understand what was happening for me.

Some of the reactions to loss may include:

- A deep feeling of sadness that seems all-encompassing.
- Often a need to shed tears.
- A feeling of, "Could this really be happening?" Shock and a feeling of numbness.
- Not sure whether we want to be alone although experiencing an intense feeling of isolation and loneliness.
- Anxious, unable to see a way forward.
- Guilty – did we do enough? Sometimes there may be guilt when relief comes into the mix.
- Feeling different – will we ever be the same?
- Trying to get on with things but an inability to concentrate.
- Feeling ill and having problems sleeping.
- Not being able to enjoy doing your usual activities.
- Finding that there can be tensions in relationships.
- Trying to dull the pain through the use of alcohol or drugs.
- The general malaise of feeling that nothing is helping – and even having suicidal thoughts.

Twelve Steps

I hope that through the stories and reflections from people in this book, you can see that there are no simple ways of getting through grief and the pain of loss. There will be a time-space when we may feel that nobody, or no particular action, can ease the intensity of our pain. There comes a time when we may feel ready to hear about what has helped others and work out what might help us. Whilst I certainly don't see grief as addictive, I am drawn to the notion of the twelve steps. So here are some steps that have been drawn from my own experiences and research:

1. **Grieving is a normal process** so allow yourself to grieve.
2. **Choose to express how you are feeling**, if you can, to someone you trust.
3. **Make sure you look after yourself.** It is amazing how therapeutic exercising is, particularly in a gym or somewhere where there are

people. I found the treadmill very freeing, even for short periods of time. Also, try to eat healthily and drink lots of water.

4. **Don't make any big decisions**. Give yourself at least a year before you tackle any major life decisions.

5. **Communicate** – Even though we may not feel like communicating, it can be important to be able to communicate to others what you feel would be helpful, because often other people don't know how to act. Let them know if you do want to talk, or if you don't. If they ask if they can help, allow them to do so in some way, but let them know how. People want to be able to help.

6. **Find something that soothes your soul.** I found that the music that I had shared with my husband was healing. Others like to have material things that remind them of their loved one. Some find it better to put things away.

7. **The importance of touch**. You may not feel like being touched, but it can be therapeutic. Hugs are good or even a massage.

8. **Allow yourself to heal.** Look at the things that are troubling you. Do you feel guilty that you might forget – we can get stuck in not being able to move on. It is a normal part of healing that we may feel unable to move on, but it is important to feel that it is possible.

9. **We can survive**. There were times that I felt I couldn't bear what I was experiencing but ultimately found that I could. Be assured that you can get through this. There will be times when you might feel you are going backwards but always know that you will survive. In fact, in time you can not only survive – you can thrive and find your fabulous again.

10. **Seek help if required**. It is not a weakness to seek professional help. Lifeline offered me free counselling which I took advantage of. I found it helpful to get outside assurance that I was on the right track.

11. **Be aware of stress triggers**. Christmas, birthdays, anniversaries and other significant events can remind us of what we have lost. It is better to be prepared that this might happen and allow yourself to feel some sadness. Sometimes the days preceding

events can be harder and the event itself may not be as hard as we were expecting because we have prepared ourselves.

12. **Be kind to yourself.** Do the things you like doing. I joined a laughing yoga course and found that it helped to get reconnected. Even though the laughing was contrived, it felt good. Try to connect with people and get involved in activities. The mood framework is a good guide to the progress you are making.

How can we help someone who is grieving?

We often don't know how to help those who are grieving. Here are a few ideas:

- **Let them know that you care.** Certainly, acknowledge their loss – don't skirt around it.
- **Let them know how you feel** – that you don't know what to say, but you will be there for them if they ever need to talk.
- **When they want to talk, be the best listener you can be** – let them know it is okay for them to share anything, even if it can be hard to witness their pain. Never play down their loss. Listen without giving advice.
- **Be aware of giving platitudes** and never say "at least".
- **Keep in touch and include them in activities** even if they decline – don't give up on them.
- **Accept that they may act differently.** Two years after my loss I bumped into someone who had previously been a good friend and had slipped away not long after my husband's death as I felt that she had found my behaviour bizarre and difficult to handle. She reluctantly agreed, but through our discussion, she began to understand and our friendship was reconnected.
- **Look for any signs that they need professional help.** Stay tuned to look out for signs that they may be feeling overwhelmed and in danger of harming themselves.

***

I have endeavoured to explore a number of different experiences with grief. Of course, there are many more, and each brings its challenge for us to find our way out. I hope that you have been inspired by the people who have shared their stories with me. It has been a real privilege to be given the opportunity to get to know these people better. None of them sees themselves as heroes, but each is the hero of their own story.

Each person mentioned in this book has indicated that answers don't always appear overnight. It is the continual searching, the notion of never giving up, the daily practices and refusing to play the blame game, including self-blame. Learning to understand and accept who we are is a vital component of our fabulous journey. I still find the mood framework such a valuable reminder for me to understand where I am at in any given situation.

I'd like to conclude with another example of how powerful it is to become better observers of ourselves and others.

For a more in-depth study of the power of moods and all of its components that enable us to live more productive lives, I would highly recommend the three volumes of Alan Sieler's books, *Coaching to the Human Soul*. They have been a valuable resource for me in cultivating the moods of Acceptance, Ambition and Wonder and have certainly helped me to cultivate gratitude, joy, compassion and lightness.

Here's to us all finding our rainbow and becoming fabulous again… again…and again!

DECLARATION	FACTICITY – Facts that we asses as unchangeable	POSSIBILITY- What we assess as changeable	UNCERTAINTY- What we cannot confidently predict
The mood of Opposition	There are things that happen in our lives that we cannot change. Each of our case studies will testify to this. When we resist this and demand that it be different, we are in danger of getting into the debilitating and often destructive mood of **Resentment** in which we have closed ourselves off from positive emotions. We simply close ourselves off from getting past the things we cannot change.	When we do not accept that things can change and we feel that the future cannot be any different to the present, the mood of **Resignation** can make us feel that any action is a waste of time. We can get into a **Yes, but ...** existence. Each of our studies was in some way given the *yes, but* scenario which could have derailed their progress. It is a mood that is very prevalent in our society. I can't do this, it's never going to be any better.	When we cannot accept that we live in an uncertain world and we keep living in a background of fear that negative events will be devastating, fearful and overwhelming, the mood which debilitates us, is one of **Anxiety** It is a very prevalent mood in today's world. We miss out on so many opportunities because of our fear. We can feel confused, hostile and threatened.
The mood of Acceptance	We can release ourselves from suffering and become powerful as have our case studies. This mood of **Acceptance** allows us to live in gratitude, joy, compassion and lightness. We need to check in with ourselves – "What is the reason we keep opposing what we know we cannot change?" What would it take to let it go so we can accept and move on to become the resourceful people we are capable of being.	Each of our studies moved through the temptation to give up and instead looked for ways to generate new possibilities. The mood of **Ambition** allowed them to look at ways that they could change the reality of their situations. Shirley's father helped her to look for something good in every situation. Each developed their own way of moving forward to take action. Changing the mantra from "Yes, but ... to let's go for it."	All of our studies displayed much courage which enabled them to move past the anxiety – the 'what if' and look at the possibilities. They were actually operating out of a mood of **Wonder**. Using this mood and their courage, they were able to look deeply at such questions as: "What will happen? What will it look and sound like? " They were able to stand back and consider the future more constructively.

ACKNOWLEDGEMENTS:

Although he has transitioned from this earthly existence, my thanks will always go to my husband Michael (Mick) Hadley who is still very much part of this book.

Once again, I would like to acknowledge Alan Sieler who has been an exceptional influence on my work. As the director of Newfield Institute, which specialises in the research and teaching of Ontology as a rigorous methodology for the development of competent professional coaches and organisational consultants. He changed my life.

I am also grateful for those who agreed to the inclusion of a portion of their story. They each could write a book about their own experiences.

Special thanks to my editor, Jacquelin Melilli who has shared wisdom that has helped to make my previous book better and now has been there for me with this one.

Big thanks to my children, Vicki, Simon, Matt, wife Bev, and grandchildren Joel, Jack, Alexandra, her partner James, and Cam who have always believed in me and love me unreservedly.

REFERENCES:

Chapter 1:

Mohandas Gandhi (1869-1948)— also affectionately known as Mahatma — led India's independence movement in the 1930s and 40s by speaking softly without anger, facing down the British colonialists with stirring speeches and non-violent protest. He was killed by a fanatic in 1948.

Wiley Dean Reed (1944–2012) was an African-American blues musician and songwriter, based in Australia, who sang and accompanied himself on the piano.

Dr Brené Brown (born November 18, 1965) is a research professor at the University of Houston. Her TED talk – The Power of Vulnerability is one of the top five viewed TED talks in the world.

Rhonda Byrne (born 1945) is an Australian television writer and producer, best known for her New Thought books, The Secret, The Power and The Magic. The Magic was the Step by step, day-by-day, 28 simple practices that helped me navigate some of my early days of grief.

Brenda Davies Born in England but now living in Zambia. Having retired from medical practice in the U.K., Brenda has a lively practice in Zambia where people come from all over the world to consult with her, have psychotherapy and healing, or stay for a few weeks to have intensive therapy. I found her workbook The Seven Healing Chakras: Unlocking Your Body's Energy, helpful to me in my early stages of grief. It is filled with step-by-step guided activities and offers a voyage of self-discovery.

Sarah Kerr: Sarah is a Death Doula and Ritual Healing Practitioner. https://soulpassages.ca/

A Family Constellation is a three-dimensional group process that has the power to shift generations of suffering and unhappiness. Founder Bert Hellinger.

Elisabeth Kübler-Ross (1926 – 2004) was a Swiss-American psychiatrist and a pioneer of near-death studies. Her book *On Death and Dying* is still held as being relevant and is often quoted. In it, she first discussed her theory of the five stages of grief – also known as the Kubler-Ross model.

Helen Adams Keller (1880 – June 1968) was an American author, political activist, and lecturer. She was the first deaf-blind person to earn a bachelor-of-arts degree.

Chapter 2:

Hay House is a publisher founded in 1984 by author Louise Hay (1026-2017), who is known for her New Thought books. The publishing house describes itself as a "mind-body-spirit and transformational enterprise".

Leon Nacson is the managing director of Hay House in Australia.

The Mood Framework: Moods and emotions are an important component of the Ontological Studies taught within The Newfield Institute. **Alan Sieler,** the founder and director, constructed the framework I have used, as a user-friendly guide to some common moods. I wrote extensively about this in my previous book.

Chapter 3:

Vascular Dementia: Is the broad term used for dementia associated with problems of circulation of blood to the brain.

Geriatrician: A geriatric physician, also called a **geriatrician,** is a medical doctor who specialises in the diagnosis, treatment, and prevention of disease and disability in older adults. Geriatric physicians are primary care doctors who are specially trained in the ageing process specialising in dementia and Alzheimer's disease.

Chapter 4:

Behavioural Optometrist: Behavioural optometry has a more holistic approach to the treatment of vision and visual perceptual problems. Practitioners believe that your visual status and the way you interpret what you see is not dependent on how clear your eyesight is. They do not diagnose dyslexia, but I certainly found them helpful in diagnosing possible causes of reading difficulties.

Dyslexia: The British **Dyslexia** Association definition describes **dyslexia** as "a learning difficulty that primarily affects the skills involved in accurate and fluent word reading and spelling" and is characterised by "difficulties in phonological awareness, verbal memory and verbal processing speed". In my experience, there are many forms, and often the student can have a high IQ yet perform below others academically.

The Tournament of Minds: This is a school competition program available through Australia, New Zealand, South Africa, Hong Kong, Thailand, India, Cambodia, Indonesia and Singapore. It is designed to encourage lateral thinking, creativity and teamwork in young people.

Thinking Sideways: A language enrichment program in six levels written by Lyn Traill to embrace different styles of learning. They are now only available in libraries.

Edward De Bono: He was the inventor of Lateral Thinking and strategic brain training. I introduced a number of his concepts with children and later in the corporate world. I used his PMI (plus, minus, interesting) successfully with Aboriginal children as a brainstorming, decision making and critical thinking tool. It gave them the opportunity to examine ideas, concepts and experiences from a range of perspectives.

Chapter 5:

Jeanette Winterson: <u>CBE </u>(born 27 August 1959) is an award-winning English writer, who became famous with her first book, <u>*Oranges Are Not the Only Fruit*</u>, a <u>semi-autobiographical novel</u> about a sensitive teenage girl rebelling against conventional values. She is also a broadcaster and a professor of creative writing at Manchester University.

Ontological Coaching: It is an extraordinarily powerful methodology for effecting change for individuals, teams and organisations. It is highly effective because it is based on a new deeply grounded and practical understanding of language, moods and conversations for behavioural and cultural transformation. (Alan Sieler)

Chapter 6:

Law of Attraction: Manifesting your destiny by firstly knowing what you want and focussing on the positive aspects of what you need, desire, or want to manifest. Positive attracts positive and negative attracts negative. It is important to understand that negative thoughts attract negative outcomes. Practising positive thoughts creates positive energy. A great space to live in.

Mardy Penrose: Mardy is a highly skilled, intuitive business coach who works with the understanding that dreams and goals are only ever dreams and goals until you form a clear-cut path of action, directing you to the ultimate achievement.

<u>www.facebook.com/pg/Mardy-Penrose-Life-CoachGoals-Strategist-</u>

Michelle Cannan: Michelle has manifested a powerful five-week virtual immersion process that teaches how unwanted life cycles are the pathway to unlocking frustrating, recurring blocks in our personal, professional and financial life. www.michellecannan.com

Chapter 7:

Autism ASD: Autism Spectrum Disorder is a condition that affects social interaction, communication, interests and behaviour. In children with ASD, the symptoms are present before three years of age, although diagnosis can sometimes be made after the age of three.

Sarah Rankin: An Ambassador Diamond with *It Works*, a home-based company.

Mind Set Coaching: An effective way to make shifts in what and how you do it in business.

Chapter 8:

Houdini: Harry Houdini was a Hungarian-born American illusionist and stunt performer, noted for his sensational escape acts.

Chapter 9:

Depression is more than just a low mood – it's a serious mental health condition (mental illness) that has an impact on both physical and mental health.

Chapter 10:

Shamanism is an ancient healing tradition and a way of life—how to connect with nature and all of creation. It promotes healing with ceremonies and pilgrimage.

Kevin Turner: Kevin is the Director of The Foundation for Shamanic Studies (FSS) in Asia, and a teaching faculty member and a field research associate. He is the author of the book, **Sky Shamans of Mongolia: Meetings with Remarkable Healers**. http://www.shamanism-asia.com/kevin/

Michael Harner: Michael Harner, who passed away in February 2018, was widely acknowledged as the world's foremost authority on **shamanism** and has had an enormous influence on both the academic and lay worlds. Started in 1979, the Foundation for **Shamanic** Studies presents the world's foremost training programs in **shamanism** and **shamanic** healing.

Chapter 11:

Phuket Cleanse: A 5-minute drive from Nai Harn Beach, Phuket Cleanse Villas offers modern accommodation with a variety of wellness programs including detox, juice cleansing and massage. Health and fitness classes are available such as yoga, Thai boxing and cardio. https://phuketfit.com

Re-birthing: This is a completely natural method using breathing techniques conducted with a trained professional. It is a type of breathwork invented by Leonard Orr. Orr proposed that correct breathing can cure disease, relieve pain and help release past trauma.

Dela Catudel: Mind & Body Breakthrough Wellness. Dela is a gifted practitioner who is highly skilled at bringing together the physical and mental aspects of change. Her re-birthing sessions are profound.

Chapter 12:

Josephine Cashman and Big River Foundation: Josephine Cashman is a Warrimay entrepreneur from New South Wales. She is the Founder, Executive Director and Managing Director of Big River Consulting Pty Ltd, Big River Impact Investments Pty Ltd and the Big River Impact Foundation Limited. Big River Impact Foundation Ltd is an Indigenous-led public benevolent institution. The Foundation is dedicated to developing business capability, economic sustainability and financial independence for Indigenous Australians through social-impact investment strategies that deliver far-reaching economic and social benefits.

Chapter 13:

Meditation: This is a practice where an individual uses a technique such as mindfulness or focusing their mind on a particular object, thought or activity to train attention and awareness and achieve a mentally clear and emotionally calm state.

Louise Geary: Louise is a gifted coach. Well known for her business, 'Activate Your Feminine', Her question: "What might be possible if you could align what you do, with who you really are? www.louisegeary.com

Chapter 14:

Chasing Enso: Tatia Power has published a series of blogs under the title of "Chasing Enso". They are worthwhile reading. They can be accessed through her Facebook page.

Taryn Brumfitt's information on her body image programs can be found at: https://bodyimagemovement.com

Chapter 16:

Spina Bifida: This is a birth defect where there is an incomplete closing of the backbone and membranes around the spinal cord. It is believed to be due to a combination of genetic and environmental factors.

Iron Lung: This is a rigid case fitted over a patient's body, used for administering prolonged artificial respiration by means of using mechanical pumps. It is not used very often today but was frequently used in the 1940s and 1950s at the height of a polio epidemic.

Chapter 17:

Cranial-Sacral Treatment: This treatment is most often carried out with the patient lying down, fully clothed, in a quiet, peaceful environment. Treatment involves a very gentle touch of the practitioner's hands. This light contact may be taken up on the Cranium (head) the Sacrum (Tail-bone) the feet, the trunk, or any other part of the body as appropriate. Treatment is generally experienced as a profound relaxation and reintegration which may pervade the whole person, physically, mentally and emotionally. It is often accompanied by a feeling of lightness and ease.

Carlos Casteneda: Born in 1925 in Peru, anthropologist Carlos Castaneda wrote a total of 15 books, which sold 8 million copies worldwide and were published in 17 different languages. His works helped define the 1960s and usher in the New Age movement. Even after his mysterious death in California in 1998, his books continue to inspire and influence his many devoted fans.

Chapter 18:

The Cambodian Kids Foundation: Is a not-for-profit organisation and a registered Cambodian NGO. The foundation aims to educate and empower the people of Cambodia through a number of projects that ensure maximum sustainability and success. All of the people who work for the foundation in Australia are 100% volunteers. They work hard for the foundation because they believe in the dream of a better Cambodia for its people, not for any financial or personal gain. http://www.cambodiankidsfoundation.com/

The Sew Good Company: The Sew Good Company creates beautiful ethical, handmade clothing while supporting Cambodian and Nepalese women in sustainable, socially responsible business. They work with small businesses in Australia, helping them to make better ethical choices when choosing which brands to carry in their stores. They want it to be easier and more affordable to make the right decisions when buying clothing. https://thesewgoodcompany.org/

Chapter 20:

DNA: This is deoxyribonucleic acid. It is contained in your body's cells. It is a double, long chain of molecules called nucleotides that tell each cell what proteins to make. The DNA itself makes up chromosomes. Most genetic ancestry tests involve the analysis of small snippets of DNA passed down only through the mother, or only through the father. These tests can identify related individuals who share a common maternal or paternal ancestor, and even where in the world people with your genetic signature live today.

Kuku Yalanji: These are an Indigenous Australian people originating from the rainforest regions of Far North Queensland and were the people I worked with for five years.

Perry Cross Foundation: The Perry Cross Spinal Research Foundation aims to facilitate, collaborate and initiate the connections and research required to find a cure for paralysis. PO Box 8244, Gold Coast Mail Centre, QLD 9726 team@pcsrf.org.au http://www.pcsrf.org.au

OTHER PUBLICATIONS
BY LYN TRAILL

Lyn Traill
Sizzling at Seventy – Victim to Victorious
(Balboa 2012)

Lyn Traill & Annabelle Symes:
Spelling is not a Health Hazard
(Longman 1995)

Lyn Traill and Annabelle Symes:
Of Course You Can Read (Longman 1997)

Lyn Traill:
Six levels of *Spelling Skills*
(Oxford University Press 1998)
Six levels of lateral thinking skills *Thinking Sideways*
(Oxford University Press 1998)
Three levels of rhyme and analogy texts-
Rhyme Your Way to Sound Reading Writing and Spelling
(Oxford University Press 2001)
Series of Reading Rhymes including *Gregory the Grump*
(Malaysian Oxford University Press 2004)
Series of children's books for *Pobblebonk* series
(Cambridge University Press 2008)

Printed in the United States
By Bookmasters